T0277253

Praise for *We Become What We Normalize: What We Owe Each Other in Worlds That Demand Our Silence*

"*We Become What We Normalize* is a carefully considered and curated collection of ideas that pushes back against the waves of despair that might otherwise overwhelm anyone who is in any way immersed and sinking into a world that increasingly feels overwhelmingly treacherous. This collection of writing is a real generosity, a light flickering in the midst of darkness."

—**Hanif Abdurraqib,** author of *A Little Devil in America* and *They Can't Kill Us Until They Kill Us*

"David Dark's *We Become What We Normalize* is essential reading right now. Beautiful writing combined with sharp discernment as Dark calls readers to reflect on our all-too-common fear and shame-based reactivity to change. In a rapidly shifting world Dark models for us all what it looks like to face our own demons with grace and rigor."

—**Lisa Sharon Harper,** president and founder of Freedom Road, and author of the critically acclaimed *The Very Good Gospel* and *Fortune: How Race Broke My Family and the World—and How to Repair It All*

"I don't easily trust Christians, and especially white American Christians, on matters of social justice (or, frankly, much of anything)—but David Dark has won my trust and admiration. In *We Become What We Normalize*, Dark models the kind of honest self-reflection and empathetic action he calls his readers to. Self-reflection isn't easy, and it's often painful. But, as Dark gently and firmly shows, that kind of radical honesty—with ourselves, about ourselves, in relation to others—can be the only thing that keeps the temptation of succumbing to our 'inner fascist' at bay, particularly for those who have the most privilege in our dysfunctional society, wracked as it is by authoritarian backlash from the Right. Fascism, as Dark puts it, 'cuts the beautiful world down to the size of our own fear,' and *We Become What We Normalize* is a manual of sorts for overcoming the 'deferential fear' that can lead us down that dark road. The book is occasionally bitingly funny, as when Dark refers to his former hero Rush Limbaugh as 'among the most powerful worship leaders in American history' and 'for three decades the de facto head of the Republican Party.' But above all, *We Become What We Normalize* is a call to truth-telling, or 'the prophetic task' of shining light on unjust systems, by one of America's most thoughtful truth-tellers, who informs us that the prophetic is 'a witness I miss if I'm only alert to incoming data that flatters me, data that won't upset me or threaten my posture and privilege.' *We Become What We Normalize* is a brave, relatable, and disarmingly intimate book, by turns confessional and convicting, anecdotal and aphoristic, and full of the wisdom drawn from an unconventional canon that Dark has constructed to inform his work—one that has room for figures as diverse as Patti Smith, Octavia Butler, William Blake, LeBron James, Fred Rogers, and Kurt Vonnegut, among others—some far less well known. As an admirer of truth-tellers who happens to hail from Vonnegut's home state of Indiana, I'd like to conclude my endorsement of Dark's book by praising him in Vonnegut's words: 'Hooray for our team.'"

—**Chrissy Stroop,** senior correspondent, *Religion Dispatches*, and columnist, *openDemocracy*

"My fellow creatures, we have been gifted with only so many turns around the sun. *We Become What We Normalize* is a plea to be brave, truthful, and joyful with our lives. In a clear and prophetic voice reminiscent of Wendell Berry and

Richard Rohr, David Dark invites us to live authentic, wholehearted, undivided lives. Sit alongside David Dark for a spell. Observe him as he disarms himself by telling the deepest truths about his life. In turn, Dark's courage and wisdom might help you disarm yourself—and thus spark a revolutionary process of generating the deep reflection and liberating love our world so desperately needs."

—Bonnie Smith Whitehouse, author of *Seasons of Wonder: Making the Ordinary Sacred through Projects, Prayers, Reflections, and Rituals*

We Become What We Normalize

What We Owe Each Other in Worlds
That Demand Our Silence

We Become
What We
Normalize

David Dark

Broadleaf Books

Minneapolis

WE BECOME WHAT WE NORMALIZE
What We Owe to Each Other in Worlds That Demand Our Silence

Scripture quotations, unless otherwise noted, are from the New Revised Standard Version Bible, copyright © 1989 National Council of the Churches of Christ in the United States of America. Used by permission. All rights reserved worldwide.

Scripture quotations marked NRSVA are from the New Revised Standard Version Bible: Anglicized Edition, copyright © 1989, 1995 National Council of the Churches of Christ in the United States of America. Used by permission. All rights reserved worldwide.

Scripture quotations marked KJV are from the King James Version. Public domain.

Lyrics to "Robot Soft Exorcism" in chapter 5 are used by permission of Dustin Kensrue.

Cover design: 1517 Media

Library of Congress Control Number 2023011485 (Print)

Print ISBN: 978-1-5064-8168-5
eBook ISBN: 978-1-5064-8169-2

Printed in India

For Bob Sherman

We're all clairvoyant if we'd only know it.
—Sophie Heywood, *The Salt Eaters,*
by Toni Cade Bambara

Contents

Introduction

Is This Thing On?

Being harmed and harming through shame

There's a thing I do that scares me. More than once, I've been behind the wheel of a vehicle at, say, a four-way stop. I've gotten so distracted that I've screwed up. I've stayed stopped too long or hit the gas too soon. I've missed my cue. Sometimes my missed cues have involved pedestrians entering a crosswalk. Avoiding grave mishaps, I've recovered myself in time, but these incidents recur. They are, I admit, a part of my life.

Here's the part that scares me more.

A time or two, I've been so ashamed over this public, verifiable vehicular error that I put the pedal to the metal to hasten my escape from the situation.

1

Ever notice somebody doing that? An audible, visible acceleration clearly born of shame? It's hard to watch, cringeworthy.

I've been that guy. I peel out, out of embarrassment at being *seen.* In that moment I'm trying to escape a form of pain, fleeing the scene of my own felt shame. By doing this, I realize I look as I feel: silly, egotistical, ignorant, and driven by ugly feelings. It's messy.

Who's making me feel so small? Nobody. Nobody to blame, really, apart from my hurried, distracted, reactive self. But my goodness, I'd sure like to blame someone. Most anyone—most any*thing*—to deflect attention anywhere but here. An awful lot of my life, if I'm not careful, can get spent anxiously (also strategically) avoiding anything that risks shame or humiliation. My reactive self *can't handle it*. My responsive and responsible self *can*. I contain multitudes.

Is this thing on?

This is a question I ask every which way. I ask it to center myself. I'm tapping the microphone of my own thoughts and feelings. I'm putting my hand over my heart, taking my temperature. I'm asking if my deepest and most creatively responsive self, my moral center, is online, available, and perhaps rising to the surface. I ask this question before speaking, driving, tweeting, signing my name, or clicking Send. I get into trouble when I don't. It's as much about my being present to the moment as it is about public interaction. It's sometimes hard to let go my ego. I emit what I admit.

Is this thing on?

I ask this question socially. I wonder aloud if I'm being heard, if the person I'm talking to is being heard, if I'm getting through, if the signals they intend are being received, if the conversation is a genuinely two-way street. The intention at work in my speech will rarely, if ever, coincide with the impact of my words, so asking the question has me taking it slow and asking how I'm being heard or if I'm hearing the other person at all. I circle back, revise aloud, listen more, back down, change and adjust my posture and position. I can apologize for what I set down less than thoughtfully earlier in the day or seconds ago or years ago.

It's when my reactive self convinces me there's no circling back *this* time that I meet trouble. I find it's hard to hear anything at all when I feel defensive or afraid.

The thing that is or isn't "on" is a lot of things. Awareness or the possibility of awareness. Consciousness or the possibility of consciousness. Movement or the possibility of movement. I think to myself *anima*, which also refers to soul, that which gives life to bodies. I go looking for it within and without: on paper, on screens, on people's faces, in sounds and voices and gestures, in design and architecture too. I look for soul—movement—in the choices people make. My choices and the choices of others.

Flustered or afraid, I hit the gas pedal and lose, in that mad moment, my sense of soul. But I get it back when I slow down and take it easy again. Turns out it didn't go anywhere. Soul is that which truly connects, the movement that sustains and supports responsive and responsible selves across distances and at intersections, the movement—*the play*—of seeing, learning, listening, and imagining myself and others well. When I'm relaxed, breathing, curious, I spy soul all around and within me, a current—a sense of play—that soothes my reactive self if I let it. Transformation is often just one smidgen or snatch of soul away.

To find courage, I seek out unflustered, unafraid people making soulful decisions, *beautiful* decisions, in news cycles, in history, in art and literature and scripture, and on the internet (as the saying goes). I collect and internalize these examples to mimic and draw inspiration from when I'm soaking in reactivity at the four-way stop and other nervy-feeling moments in my everyday doing and saying. When I hit a snag or get to feeling somehow stymied, thinking of and recalling playful people, at the right moment, puts my heart and soul back in play and makes it more likely that I'll be able to proceed through all manner of intersections without disrespecting, debasing, or disgracing myself. With their assistance, I can occasionally proceed through life with attention and caution, curiosity and style.

Are You Everybody?

In 1979, the artist Patti Smith was the guest on a Sunday-morning children's variety show called *Kids Are People Too*. And thankfully, her appearance has made its way onto YouTube, so we can access and analyze it from here on out. When you watch the recording, it's clear that, with a live studio audience of screaming young people, host Michael Young gets a bit flustered. In her brief appearance, Smith takes questions, discusses Maria Callas, "the field of rock and roll," and wanting to become a missionary as a child. What strikes me about her guest spot, however, is her playfully punchy responses to Michael Young's awkward attempt to welcome her and get the ball rolling.

"Patti, I have to start with something . . . Everybody says, 'Patti Smith, *punk rock*—'"

Immediately interrupting him, she asks, "Who? Who said it? Who said that?" And then, more pointedly, "Are *you* everybody?"

Thrown off his game, Young confirms he, for one, has said it and then turns to the audience for, well, help. They offer cheers of support for "punk rock" as a consensus identifier. Smith nods with a wry smile and reluctantly concedes that yes, punk rock is "one of the fifty thousand" ways she sees herself. But her chutzpah, her demand for specificity, her poetic puncturing of a generalization ("Are *you* everybody?") lingers long past that short clip.[1]

In the video, I see Smith modeling something ancient and essential. Young's assigned task is to maintain momentum and avoid dead air. Smith instinctively understands that meaning is a consensual activity, that idle chatter shorn of referent exacts a cost. She's polite, but she refuses to give in without a fight and brings the quick-witted moral vigilance of a righteously unmanageable person. She will sniff out and call out that which doesn't smell or sit right in her presence. She isn't inclined to abide or let slip past her, in a moment like this and in front of children, an unexamined word.

Too much is at stake.

There is, perhaps, a time to "get with the program," but there is also such a thing as *too* smooth and *too easily* soothed. Most who play host in front of a live studio audience may try to relieve the tension of an unfamiliar person with a hasty introduction that renders their presence more palatable. But heavy is the head that wears the crown of the host or hall monitor. Erring on the wrong side of fabricated ease can reduce a person, cutting them down to the size of someone else's unimaginative expectations. Persons, meanwhile, are not reducible to our ideas about them. They take time, creativity, and due reverence.

Little inaccuracies deployed to relieve tension add up into inauthentic environments and unsafe spaces. Patti Smith, like other poets and prophets, is practiced in the work of *not* relieving tension but instead dwelling within it, holding space and seeing what might come of not trying to explain it away. This is the art of creative noncompliance. For Smith, "this thing," these things, are *on.* She's going to play human and see what happens—no matter what. With her singular voice, she holds and conjures a space in which everyone is invited to artfulness, to new, unexpected, and impromptu forms of play. By being so consistently and relentlessly her most creative self, she invites us to use our voices too.

People, it turns out, have the moral power to wrest a vibe, a scene, a neighborhood, a city back from the abusive strategies of reactive and poised-to-please people. What's more, with persistence and long pauses, with the right story, song, analogy, or joke, a reactive person can become a responsive person. As one who occasionally freaks out at intersections, I undertake this transformation many times a day. Without artfulness, well, I'll be damned. Transformative possibilities are my only hope. With any luck, I'll remain awake and alive to them in the days remaining to me. Is this thing on?

Surviving as a Human Being

More than one person in my life has helped me feel and access my own moral power and get curious and creative over my conflicts, my own stupefied moments. At our best, we lean into and respond to tension instead of ignoring or repressing it. Ignoring that which makes us uncomfortable, and repressing the fact of it, is a reactive mindset. Over a few habit-forming days, weeks, or years, it can add up to the active suppression of conscience. Before we know it, a reactive personality resistant to incoming data has formed. That might sound dramatic, but a moment's consideration of what we've beheld and experienced within the first quarter of the twenty-first century might serve as evidence.

I start small to go big later. I begin with myself and the things I do that scare me. Contemplating my own, not-infrequent anxiety at intersections helps me have a little more compassion for the powerfully positioned people whose reactivity I see—beholding my own reflection—in news feeds. I am not so different. I, too, do more than occasional disservice to my own humanity when I'm afraid and flustered. Reactivity is a pattern in my own life reflected in patterns in the larger world. Something akin to the macro-level reactivity of autocrats and oligarchs and their enablers can be easily discerned in my bad driving habits. We are, after all, everyone else. The personal is universal.

But then there are people like Patti Smith all around me, people who insist on conceiving themselves and others creatively and responsively, which is to say poetically. When I sit with my conflicted feelings, consider what data they might yield, and accept tension as essential to longed-for transformation, I begin to become, in some sense, the Patti Smith I'm looking for, someone who chooses acknowledgement over avoidance.

Parker Palmer has a dramatic word for what conflict avoidance costs us: "If the end of tension is what you want, fascism is the thing for you."[2] Home is where the hurt is, but it doesn't stay there. Feelings cascade into behaviors. We might imagine the cost of a misspoken, reactive word is small, but it yields harm. Fascism cuts the beautiful world down to the size of our own fear. If I'm skilled at preemptively easing tension with easily tossed out words and gestures, preventing and policing the curiosity that might otherwise lead to moral realization about myself and others, I'm skilled at fascism. It could even be said that I have a knack for it.

I'm not a fascist. But I have an inner fascist (likely you do too) to contend with. I feel it at intersections literal and figurative. My reactive self (hello, inner fascist) is often debilitatingly uncomfortable with one issue intersecting with another. But issue silos are fictions that dissolve upon contact with the sweet, social fact of relationship—and there's no escape from relationship. Every fact is a function *of* relationship. Good news for bullies: a bullying train of feeling—like a bullying train of thought—can be stopped. We can freeze the frame and slow the tape.

Best to lean into the tension and ask for specificity. I'm going to need an inner Patti Smith or three to undertake this work. To not be useful in the strategies of abusive people, including, sometimes, me. Is this thing on?

"If you can form close human attachments to those around you, you have the possibility of surviving as a human being."[3] That's Fanny Howe describing the hoped-for possibility and the stakes. With close human attachments, we can hear and be heard and locate ourselves among other sometimes-anxious selves craving reality. We can learn. When we're afraid we tend to defer to whatever authority we imagine might momentarily relieve us of our fear. Deferential fear dictates our speech, our behavior, and our sense of what's possible.

Deferential fear rules the state, the head, and the heart. Except when it doesn't. Asking the question that refuses the easy answer is the slow, steady, even sometimes sudden overcoming of deferential fear. It happens all the time where two or more are gathered, where honest, human contact occurs, when we get personal and play human.

Decisions Create Culture

"That was weird, right?" is one helpful variation of *Is this thing on?* The commonplaceness of these expressions reminds us that in moments of debrief, morally serious people everywhere entertain questions like these. They do so after meetings, parties, classes, visits with family, weddings, funerals, transactions in public places, or watching a knucklehead speed away in shame after sitting at a four-way stop a few seconds too long. The questions appear, signaling, conjuring comment and further inquiry: *Is this thing on?* "That was weird, right?"

If even one other person has the will and wits to affirm in response, "Yes, that was weird," a small school of thought forms, an opening occurs, and a perhaps debilitating silence ends. Fascism has been broken, and a tiny bit of ground has been won against something big or small that seemed off. Depending on the context, the space afforded by such observational candor can serve as a sign of life, a small step toward something more dramatic and consequential: "That wasn't appropriate. . . . Something is wrong. . . . Time to stand up."

Is this thing on? I'm trying to describe the very small but enormously consequential moves with which a person makes their witness in the world, standing in integrity and holding the doors of perception open. Deciding to bear witness may begin with a resolve to hold in true tension what occurred and is occurring. Remembering rightly is a little decision. But when multiplied, it adds up to the very big and beautiful decisions that come into view with words like *freedom* and *civilization* and *justice* and *culture*.

Beautiful decisions are all around us. They add up, despite the catastrophically ugly, evasive, and reactionary decisions that—we know feelingly—also add up. Decisions create culture.

That's not my line. I borrowed "Decisions create culture" from a friend, Nashville-based psychologist Christina Edmondson.[4] Owning small, unworthy choices as actual, deliberate decisions can feel draining and exhilarating all at once when they affect everyone, as they do.

In an effort to urge my multiple selves to own our own bullshit, I remember my "not a big deal" *is too* a big deal because decisions create culture. My decisions and the decisions of others.

That three-word aphorism, applied widely and consistently, personally and publicly, goes a long way toward getting a fix on fate. Or arresting—and possibly reversing—the sinking feeling of the inevitable. If decisions create culture, perhaps what *is* isn't what has to be.

The Holy Work of Situational Awareness

Injustice isn't an accident. It's a setup. It's orchestrated. Tiny betrayals of self and others add up and cascade into calamity and an accompanying climate of fear. But little rituals of remembrance and setting something aright, of self-regard and the regard of others, add up too. Small, meaningful actions can change the course of human events.

We have before us, for instance, the courageous witness of an unnamed and unarmed man who confronted and obstructed the advance of a column of Type 59 tanks in Beijing on June 5, 1989. As the tank crew tried to maneuver around him, footage shows this bold individual—now known as "Tank Man"—adjusting his position to block their path at every turn. He was seized and whisked away with his briefcase, and his fate and whereabouts remain unknown. Rumor has it similar moves, lost to history, also occurred among pro-democracy demonstrators in Tiananmen Square.

But the photo and footage of Tank Man's action moved the needle of our geopolitical scene and continue to inspire contemplation and accompanying artfulness. Something essential was fostered in his revolutionary decision, his impromptu act of civic courage. Man versus mechanism. One human being made a poetic and prophetic appeal to the conscience of those present as well as the watching world. A culture of repression was decisively and graphically confronted. Something was cultivated and set in motion when Tank Man made his witness.

These moves, publicized and unpublicized, occur somewhere each and every day. Consider Bree Newsome and an ugly flag in South Carolina. Consider Jesus of Nazareth and his cross.

The fact of the matter is this: we're never not cultivating culture in one way or another. It all matters. Every move. Scary and true.

There's a culture developing between us right now. Read these words aloud in someone's hearing and something different (but also related) will be cultivated. Is this thing on?

This is the holy work of situational awareness, of knowing what we're up to, of being where we live and experiencing consciously the dramas that are otherwise enacted upon us unconsciously. Ask not if you're in a cult. Ask this: Which ones?

This book is about the stuff we put ourselves and others through. It's a deep dive into my own struggle with deferential fear, which I see mirrored in the experiences of others and in the news cycles we behold as we doom scroll, taking in cult-creating words, images, and signals about our surrounding worlds. They are a part of me. Of us.

Our evasions and the evasions of others yield, with humiliating exactness, the cultures, the systems, we're in. We become what we normalize. And we create, sometimes haplessly, sometimes purposefully, cultures that normalize more than a little dysfunction, more than a little toxicity and terror and trauma. Have you noticed? Is this thing on?

We're surrounded and hemmed in by structures of concentrated reactivity that exhaust and deplete us as well as structures that serve as legacies of moral responsibility. In time, I'll invite you to conceive these structures as robots over whom we have more control than we're prone to imagine. We need not be forever stuck in the hopeless reactivity of others. We can chart a different course. I have analyses and strategies to share alongside a serving of confession and the sometimes-unflattering data of my own life. It gets weird.

I believe and hope to demonstrate that deferential fear can be overcome. The work is personal and political, internal and cultural every which way. It *is* being overcome here and there and everywhere. Yes, there are myriad meltdowns, but there is also an abundance of underpublicized breakthroughs. I mean to document a few in these pages.

Here again, Patti Smith, our living authority in self-regard, right remembering, and creative consciousness, has words for the assignment I'm taking up: "Social media, in its twisting of democracy, sometimes courts cruelty, reactionary commentary, misinformation, and nationalism, but it can also serve us. It's in our hands. The hand that composes a message, smooths a child's hair, pulls back the arrow and lets it fly."[5]

I intend my memories, my analyses, and my analogies contained here as arrows "aiming for the common heart of things," to again borrow Smith's words.[6] I offer them as a sometimes-clumsy summons to attentiveness, risky goodness, and group courage. I'm trying to hold space.

Patti Smith isn't the only person who has a knack for stopping a train of thoughtlessness. Others have managed that feat and will again. We can too.

1

Peer Pressure Is Forever

Courage, conscience, and deferential fear

About eighteen years ago, I was in New York City at just the right moment to visit just the right friend who knew just the right person to get us on the guest list for the after-party that followed the broadcast and taping of an episode of *Saturday Night Live*. This prospect was an absolute dream come true, the golden ticket of a lifetime for me. I was so excited I could hardly contain myself.[1]

Even as a child I loved recalling and reenacting SNL skits at school on Monday mornings. SNL marked an expansion of the space of the talk-aboutable. It was available evidence of lived freedom, alive and signaling, long before I knew, exactly, what

17

comedy was. So what could be cooler and more promising than hanging out with the cast and other special someones who possessed the secret password to join the party?

Entering the venue felt a little like walking into a scene from Stanley Kubrick's *Eyes Wide Shut*. The room was dimly lit. Everyone was chatty, smiling, animated, and expensively clothed. I couldn't help but feel an air of soft intimidation. For me, available ease was in short supply. From dreaming I might casually pal around or strike up a conversation with Fred Armisen or Amy Poehler, I suddenly knew, feelingly, that to even try to initiate some friendly banter with any famous person who didn't know me already would expose me as an outsider.

I'd longed my whole life long to not be out of my element at a moment like this. Reader, I was out of my element.

The entourage within which I arrived was soon fused with the entourage of our host. Introductions were made. The noise level made conversation next to impossible. When a server appeared to take drink orders, this father of three panicked and ordered the same kind of beer as the person next to me. I didn't want to do or say *anything* that might out me as not belonging there. That's weird, right?

I strained to hear what others were saying and tried to chime in, if memory serves, with how much I, like our host, *also* admired Tom Waits. But feeling paralyzed by a desire to successfully audition for friendship with fame had me tongue-tied, actively throwing away my perceived shot at popular significance. I *felt* inappropriate, and, like the driver at the intersection, willing to do almost anything to feel like I wasn't, to weigh in and change my personality into whatever shape might fit the occasion.

In no time at all, it was time to leave and to pay for my beer. I was assured, in a hushed tone, that our host had picked up the tab. How nice of him! How opportune for me. This gave me occasion to address him more personally and directly.

"Thanks for the drink," I said, knowing I'd made a bonehead move, outing myself as a mere civilian as soon as the words came out. He fixed a bored, glassy stare on me that seemed to pay me more mind than I'd gotten all evening. I began to feel like someone's liability, a real hayseed, an embarrassment. *Of course* the person among us who'd just appeared on live television had paid for drinks.

"You're welcome," he assured me. It felt like a door closing. I would not be exchanging contact information with a member of the cast of *Saturday Night Live*. The ladder I'd hoped to ascend vanished before me. I felt slighted and dwarfed as shame blossomed within me.

This awkward exchange with a famous person I would never lay eyes on again isn't an indictment of anyone or anything in particular, but something wasn't on. Gripped by social anxiety, trying to read a room and dwell meaningfully within it, I didn't much like what the room told me about myself and my tender ego.

My story is about loose ends, the alluring currency of access, and, most of all, the catastrophic operation of deferential fear at work, which I've been slow to see among allegedly powerful and publicly talkative people around the world. Peer pressure, I've come to know feelingly, is forever. And it builds and diminishes our cultures each and every day.

The Active Suppression of Conscience

Consider this. In October 2016, the American public was made privy to an *Access Hollywood* audio recording of then candidate Donald Trump offering a detailed, gloating, and graphic description of his own act of sexual assault. "When you're a star," he explains, "they let you do it."[2]

For a day or two, his status as the standard-bearer of the Republican Party was in doubt. Paul Ryan disinvited Trump to a campaign rally.[3] Mike and Karen Pence went radio silent. Difficult decisions confronted the cast of brand GOP. Surely this was a dealbreaker. How could the campaign, or anyone associated with it, continue under this dark cloud?

There were emerging indicators, however, of a power dynamic that seemed to counsel against decoupling. Paul Ryan discovered that, absent Trump, he was a thin stage presence at his own rally. In an impromptu news conference arranged by Steve Bannon on the night of the second debate, Trump seated to his left and to his right accusers of Bill Clinton: Juanita Broaddrick, Paula Jones, Kathleen Willey, and Kathy Shelton. Following Bannon's lead, Trump narrated the scene: "These four very courageous women have asked to be here, and it was our honor to help them."[4]

That was weird, right? It was an eye-rubbingly strange sight. Yes, Donald Trump stood accused and unrepentant as a sexual assailant, but behold these women who'd been treated like pariahs for years, whose allegations against Bill Clinton—we were made to visually recall—were never disproven. The people of the United States of America were being dramatically reminded of a certain sustained hypocrisy of predatory behavior in high places, which many Americans had, admittedly, made a kind of peace with, perhaps through repression, not long ago. After they each shared statements of support for Donald Trump, reporters who tried to ask about the *Access Hollywood* tape were shouted down by Paula Jones: "Why don't y'all go ask Bill Clinton that? Go ahead. Ask Hillary as well."[5]

And with that, the very pattern of moral evasiveness Steve Bannon sought to forcibly recall to our minds through public staging was set to repeat. The fact of what we'd heard and knew began to be somehow squared away by a set of conflict-avoidant high rollers. Within hours, everyone on Team Trump was, by all appearances, back on board.

There would be occasional hiccups. During Betsy DeVos's confirmation hearing, for instance, Senator Patty Murray asked her, under oath, if DeVos would characterize the actions Trump described on the tape as sexual assault. "Yes," she replied.[6] Needless to say, this didn't cause her to conscientiously decline an appointment by Donald Trump. And no one I know of publicly suggested she should. The loose end, smoothed over by DeVos, followed a norm set by others serving in that administration, every candidate for public office who received Trump's endorsement, everyone who stood up to applaud him as he entered a room, and, needless to say, millions of American voters.

Does the exercise of power require the active suppression of conscience? It is important we refrain from trying to answer too quickly. We don't have to be famous or hold elected office to meaningfully mull the social fact of access and what a precious commodity it is in every facet of life within our human barnyard.

We Become What We Sit Still For

Our lives consist of certain trade-offs. Many of us learn to skim past certain facts, certain people, particular data we imagine might doom us in our effort to gain and maintain what we believe we need to live, rather than registering or acknowledging them aloud. Rather than asking, *Is this thing on?* we act, speak, and, to a large degree, see and think within the lines dictated by the perceived necessity of maintaining our overhead. We often turn the apparatus off, studiously avoiding upsetting the wrong people. Think of abusive people you suspect you can't afford to risk personally upsetting. Think of Joe Biden fist-bumping Mohammed bin Salman.

Honoring and remaining fully alive to your own conscience is the human assignment. But it's especially difficult if you make your coin declining to go quite that far at every turn. Whether at home or at work or within any of the arrangements that make up our existence, humans learn to banish our awareness of certain facts into a hidden compartment of the mind to make momentary peace with whomever we have to. In America, many of us feel free to say what we see and remember aloud what we remember, but only up to a point.

Moving past that point is the risk of drama and the privilege of comedy. Both serve as a form of catharsis, and both, at their most intense, can be difficult to categorize. This was the dark power on display when Steve Bannon single-handedly commandeered the news cycle with the sight he successfully staged. Even now, when I recount that moment to people who followed it, they look at me as if I've brought up a long-repressed memory. We don't want to know what we don't want to know until we do. And we're alarmingly skilled at repressing what we didn't want to know to begin with. Even if the cost is exacted out of sight, a price is paid for our repressions.

The presence of these popularly forgotten aggrieved women on national television shocked our systems with a narrative zoom out. It played to latent guilt and dread in the American psyche. Had everyone who'd applauded or partnered with Bill Clinton been complicit in normalizing abuse all along?

That moment proved our popular memory is highly selective, privileging some testimonies over others, passing over, sidelining, and consigning to a kind of social death people whose truth doesn't fit the narratives of what we want to believe about ourselves. Needless to say, some narratives are more crushingly well funded than others. Some abusers are peculiarly well protected against moral oversight.

We were in for more of the same. "What an idiot," Alec Baldwin's Donald Trump mused aloud on SNL concerning the fate of convicted millionaire sexual predator Harvey Weinstein. "He could have gotten away with all of it if only he'd gotten himself elected president."[7]

Given what we've seen and experienced over the last decades, the alliances that have held despite every betrayal of the public good, this grimly candid conclusion concerning the moral debasement most career Republicans would undergo to stay in the game, protecting their president from every form of moral accountability at every turn, is hard to deny.

My brief evening in a shared space with cast members of *Saturday Night Live* was only unique in the sense that my experience offered a level of casual access to fame and fortune I hadn't encountered before and haven't stumbled into since. And it speaks to the question of access and the suppression of conscience some forms of access seem to require.

The memory of the evening has surfaced in recent years as I've tried to conjure feelings of empathy for elected officials and other public figures, millionaires but also some billionaires, who've opted to suppress their own conscience repeatedly instead of risking specific words of public candor that might cost them their seats or their perceived standing.

They appear to be set for life and are arguably among the freest people the world has ever seen, and yet a spirit of deferential fear appears to have dictated their every public move down to today. How did this happen?

We become what we sit still for, what we play along with, and what we abide even as we hold on to what we have (or think we have). A risk averseness, if we aren't careful, can cost us our own capacity to *be moved.* This, of course, is our capacity for love, arguably, our soul. We become what we normalize.

If association is currency, we're perhaps prone to mistake the trades we make to keep accruing it with leadership and prestige and success and even realism. Making that trade-off, what is truly essential is lost on us. We're hollowed out. We lose the ability, in Toni Cade Bambara's phrase, "to get basic with each other."[8] We gain a world of alleged security but only through frittering away our soul (anima), that which reminds us we are human beings among human beings—kin—bound by obligations of decency. If we don't nurture readiness to risk something for someone else's good, soul leaves us (or we estrange ourselves from it). Kurt Vonnegut sets a warning out for us when we spy this path: "We are what we pretend to be, so we must be careful about what we pretend to be."[9]

Bystander Effect

In September 2020, Bob Woodward made headlines when he shared recordings of Donald Trump recognizing aloud in February the deadly threat the coronavirus posed ("This is deadly stuff") and describing in March his decision to publicly deny the threat ("I wanted to always play it down").[10] The decision to keep the country in the dark to his own lonely advantage instead of taking decisive, but politically unpopular, action was roundly condemned. But what of Bob Woodward? What did he owe his fellow Americans when he heard and recorded the president—*our* president—speaking these words early that spring?

Like John Bolton, he had a book coming out. The common obligations of decency don't stop at the doorstep of power and fame. In deference to his own perceived personal advantage, Bob Woodward declined to pull the fire alarm.

Reality Winner saw a threat to our election integrity over six years ago and took action by leaking classified material to the Intercept. When she did, she was muzzled and incarcerated by the United States government for four years. Why no book tour for her? Why isn't her act of conscience talked about? Or the price she's paying for it?

Deferential fear. That default setting within the pundit class that leaves millions of Americans with a limited media diet and steers clear of data that upsets the status quo. The disinclination to risk loss of ad revenue gives us talking heads who know what it takes to persist in the public eye. They know how to avoid being seen as folks who won't play ball. To be perceived as overly biased, political, or polarizing is to lose access to airtime.

Nobody wants to kill the vibe. Nobody wants to be perceived as difficult or, as the saying goes, divisive. Woodward and Bolton, high rollers, are permitted to play so long as they strategically decline to risk the baseline moral seriousness of mere mortals. When you're a star, you get to. In the land of the free, we center some and sideline others. Decisions create culture.

Reality Winner's act of conscience made her a loose end, a liability, a decorated veteran with a strange name who, it appears, almost every elected official in the United States and most public figures have studiously avoided publicly acknowledging for years. Some forms of observational candor and civic courage are more costly for some than others.

Do you recognize the phenomenon of deferential fear? Have you observed it playing out in your own nervous system?

I have. It is. Ubiquitous and chronically underestimated, deferential fear puts us at war with our best, freest selves. Deferential fear saps us of any trust we might have in our own intuition, our truest perceptions, and our truest judgments. It also estranges us from our own voices, our own moral power, and a sense of our own agency. It renders us feckless and afraid in the face of injustice.

"You're always waiting for somebody else to speak up. It's that bystander effect."[11] That's Reality Winner on one form deferential fear assumes. If others know and see what's happening, perhaps they'll step in and say something so we don't have to. On May 9, 2017, Winner overcame it and lost four years of her life for her act of conscience. Woodward and Bolton, when it mattered, did not. It is my hope that she'll have libraries named after her. How do we become people who won't succumb to the bystander effect?

True learning—in the most righteous sense—is, as bell hooks tells us, the practice of freedom, made possible by "teaching that enables transgressions."[12] Practiced freedom involves feats of courage and attentiveness despite the predominance of that hovering deferential fear.

If the Yiddish proverb is true, and the heart *is* half prophet, perhaps it can only be accessed with the affection of others, those who help us heal the other half that's often too bullied and anxious to know its own worth. We're often overwhelmed, in the American context, by the drive to hurry up and matter, the drive to stay ahead. And headed where, exactly?

We get to ask ourselves this question anew each day. What place are we hoping to get to by playing it safe in the stories we tell and the voices we amplify? What spot do we hope to hold by declining to say what we see?

If the price of admission within my peer group is the frequent suppression of my own conscience, I wish to assert that the price is too high.

"It's always easier not to think for oneself. Find a nice safe hierarchy and settle in. . . . It's always easiest to let yourself be governed."[13] That's Ursula K. Le Guin's character Bedap naming the appeal of the bystander effect and the moral challenge of self-governance in one short passage. Thinking and acting critically and independently, assuming responsibility for our own imaginations, our own sayings and doings, can feel too burdensome, too triggering, and too costly. Playing along to get along can feel easier, but it's no way to live. We become what we cave to. We must be very careful about what we cave to.

How do I honor and heed the prophet within me when my fear compels me to keep it all hid? One brave and risky conversation at a time. "It is the reality of personal relationships that saves everything,"[14] Thomas Merton writes. To believe this is to consciously involve ourselves in the lives of others, to hold a sacred conception of culture where the evasion of conscience and the avoidance of conflict are never acceptable means to some other end. There are people and persons to think about. Lives are at stake. Theirs matter as much as ours. They aren't expendable. They have so much to show us. There are no randos.

What does the saving reality of personal relationships require of us? It requires we don't let deferential fear do our thinking for us. This is the challenge even when we aren't confronting an insurrection involving elected officials and political appointees refusing to concede in a presidential election. It appears before us in myriad settings throughout our lives: the pressure to keep the peace that *is* no peace.

Our presumed consent functions as a free pass for abuse. "What demon possessed me that I behaved so well?" Thoreau once asked himself.[15] In the land of the free, what do I owe people whose lives are endangered by my silence? We are not without resources. Courage, it often turns out, is contagious. *Group* courage is righteously intoxicating. Others have been here before. Come together. Education, the practice of freedom, is forever.

2

What Do You Do with the Mad That You Feel?

Feelings as mentionable and manageable

As a twenty-year-old with a long commute to college and an AM car radio, I developed an unhealthy attachment to the thinking of Rush Limbaugh. He was funny and confident, and employing his arguments aloud to others made me feel strong. More often than not, I was repeating his talking points without letting myself realize they were his and not mine. But the thought of his voice helped me hold my head a little higher in sociology class.[1]

Rush—or my idea of Rush—made me feel strong whenever I felt belittled by history, other people's thoughtfulness, and other forms of available data. He helped me believe the anxiety I felt when confronted by the fact of other people was about *them*, not me. When I was tired of feeling outsmarted, he helped me feel smart again, like an espresso shot of perceived righteousness. He scratched an itch.

In the early nineties, I remember David Letterman concluding an episode of the *Late Show* by announcing that Rush Limbaugh was going to be his guest the next evening. His studio audience erupted with cheers *and* boos. Letterman looked flustered and made a joke about how unexpected that was.

This was exciting. Here was a new thing among us. An emerging celebrity who didn't fit available categories. Rush was entering the mainstream. For a young man like me, this was a sign that perhaps my own perceived quirkiness would also find a home. I'd had the same feeling watching Elvis Costello and Andy Kaufman. From here, Rush's own television show took off, and . . . this was the beginning of the end. For me anyway.

I'd felt energized by the sound of his voice, his language, his quick-wittedness, and the way he made short work of anyone who opposed him. But having a face to look at . . . actually watching him do his thing—the derision, the mockery, the contempt, the bullying—made me ashamed to be associated with him. Reactivity is more convincing on the radio.

Watching it manifest and have its way with a human nervous system is harder to stomach.

He had, however, taught me that I own the White House, that I'm responsible for what my taxes pay for (drone strikes, golf trips, Congressional Medals of Honor) and all that my government does with my presumed consent. In America, what the government undertakes with my presumed consent is, in a deep sense, on me. Hortense Spillers and Howard Zinn would also show me this, but Rush came first. He also turned me on to Snapple.

I could name seventy-five friends and family members who have given more of their emotional lives to Rush Limbaugh's words than they've given to their spawn, their spouses, or their parents. In this sense, he was among the most powerful worship leaders in American history. Media pundits, like Letterman then and now, seem to remain at a loss for words in describing what his witness means even though he was, for three decades, the de facto head of the Republican party. There's a pattern. Reactivity is ratings gold. Trump didn't start the fire.

Anger, Vampire Weekend tells us, wants a voice.[2] This is true. My anger found one in Rush Limbaugh until it didn't. When I try to reckon how I began to break free of his—or his product's—hold, I remember other enthusiasms I held in those years that rendered me less hopeless and less obviously deferential to a network of bigotry.

I also liked Dostoevsky and Public Enemy and R.E.M., and this increased my chances of not estranging myself in the company of thoughtful people. There was also *Star Trek* and *Doctor Who* and comic books. Most blessedly, a sufficient number of my teachers and companions refused to hold my Limbaugh-dependent speech against me and, out of kindness, minimized my less-toxic quirks. They gave me the gift of imagining there was more to me than my strange opinions, which I now see were often at and even past the point of hardening into abusive positions. I do not know where I would be without such kindness.

Artisans of Moral Seriousness

These days, I try to pay this kindness forward by impersonating a teacher for a living. I describe my job this way to avoid shame and embarrassment. In what is surely the most insanely presumptuous task undertaken by any member of our species, I dare to try to help people with their own thinking. I sit in rooms with women and men in prisons and college campuses, and, together, we make assertions, put questions to one another, tell stories, read poems aloud, and wonder over our words.

My job, as I understand it, is to help people pay deep attention to their deepest selves in relationship with other selves. They write sentences. I write sentences next to their sentences. And we get a conversation going somehow. For some students, I sometimes have the feeling that this might be the first time someone has calmly and respectfully urged them to think twice. I hope it isn't the last.

I write Kendrick Lamar lyrics on the board. His rights and his wrongs, he tells us, he'll *write* till he's *right* with God.

I'm trying to conjure a sacred space of responsiveness in a sea of reactivity. To my surprise, even those who profess love for Kendrick Lamar are surprised to see words they've overheard on speakers or internalized via playlists written out like a mission statement. But pop songs often contain a righteous motto, a mental health strategy. I suggest, and most agree with me, that these words—this testimony—signal an exceedingly sound ethical commitment.

It's something of a sneak affirmation attack. I want them to know that *philosophy*—the active love of wisdom—is perhaps closer to their own lives and listening habits than they might initially assume. Poetry, that which makes things new, is too. Maybe they already love and collect it. Their relationship to both, I say, began long before we appeared before one another in a classroom. Who wants in on the thoughtfulness party? I do. Maybe you do too. Kendrick Lamar, Phoebe Bridgers, and all kinds of other people we already find amazing are waiting for us. Shall we join them again, one more time?

Critical thinking, we call it in the classroom. I don't want to call it "critical theory" until they know that *theory* just means thought. Some have been told by their parents and other politicians that critical theory is bad and critical race theory is even worse. "Thoughtfulness party" or, better, "beloved community"[3] or "group courage" or "artisans of moral seriousness" sometimes does a better job of setting a table for impressionable young people.

To paraphrase early Wilco, we get to be people who insist on finding the time to write our minds the way we want them read, people who want to be true.[4] Should we accept the mission of becoming and remaining philosophers, we'll be individuals who want to know what's true more than we want to feel successful or right or powerful. We'll desire honesty more than we desire winning. Or, as Gift of Gab of Blackalicious tells us, domination doesn't dignify diction.[5]

Lupe Fiasco once observed unto Cornel West that if he lies in a song and sells a million records, he's told a million lies.[6] Eyes widen. Are we interested in being *that* conscious of what we're up to? Do we want in on this act? Is finding out what's true and sharing it *that* much of a commitment for any of us in the here and now?

If it is, we'll be collectors of lyrics and sounds, stories and jokes, arguments and analogies that enliven our minds instead of deadening them, that illuminate the facts instead of obscuring them. We will be among those who, throughout history, have hungered and thirsted after the righteousness of cosmic plainspeak. It's a lifelong learning and yearning best undertaken in the company of others.

Urging upon people a love of liberating arts (often called a liberal arts education) is my full-time song and dance, and thoughtfulness is what I understand as a living community in which I myself am initiated anew whenever someone introduces me to another thoughtful person by way of a link, a reading recommendation, or a video. "You should check this out" is my love language. We get to set out the table of intellectual hospitality to one another in countless ways all day long. It's one of the joys of my life that I get to do it in a classroom as a paying gig, a doing unto others that which has been done unto me throughout my life and, I pray, will continue to be done from here on out.

Awareness Campaign

In a class called First Year Seminar each fall semester, we consider together Octavia Butler's *Kindred*, a novel in which a black woman, Dana, is periodically pulled back in time to the antebellum South to save the life of her white slave-owning ancestor, Rufus, at various stages of his existence. It's a life-threatening rescue operation, for herself and the enslaved community she comes to love, every single time. Saving him the first time when he's a child about to drown is easy enough, but as he ages and gradually conforms to the white supremacist terror regime that is his norm, her commitment to save him and even attempt to educate him against all odds becomes increasingly problematic.

"Not all children let themselves be molded into what their parents want them to be," she says at one point, hoping aloud.[7] But what chance does anyone have of overcoming the murderous ideas upon and within which they're raised? How do we bring ourselves (or anyone) to a realization that the world that is isn't the world that has to be? If we get there at all, even for a moment, how do we remain true to that realization once the moment has passed? As Dana observes, "a lifetime of conditioning could be overcome, but not easily."[8]

With humor and horror, the novel examines this process every which way, but, as you might guess, it ends very sadly. "I want to know why you wanted us to read this," an incarcerated mentor in my classroom once asked. I stumbled around defensively for a few minutes and eventually landed on a rationale. Like any excellent science fiction, *Kindred* can kick-start conversations about those things we've normalized and why and what it might mean to try to turn those things around. We'll always have our own ignorance to contend with, but Butler dramatizes how we can't even begin to do that without also addressing the militant ignorance of others, the reigning normalizations, and the infrastructure of bad thinking we're born into, reared within, and which we often unwittingly fund with our silence, our speech, our actions, our inaction. William Blake refers to what we're dealing with as mind-forged manacles.[9] Don't believe everything you breathe, Beck admonishes.[10] How do we even begin to decolonize our own imaginations?

In an almost comically sad scene, Dana manages to bring a book on the history of slavery back in time and places it before Rufus as a part of his continuing education. If she can make him see the world to come before it's too late, she reasons, he might become less likely to torture the people he holds captive and more likely to give his own children their freedom.

"This is the biggest lot of abolitionist trash I ever saw!" he exclaims as he reads about Sojourner Truth.

"No it isn't," she says. "That book wasn't even written until a century after slavery was abolished."

"Then why the hell are they still complaining about it?"[11]

When we discuss this exchange in class, the dots appear before us already connected. We've heard it all before. We know about the effort to ban the teaching of history in these United States with words like *critical* and *race* and *theory*. We know that disinformation is a business model.

This is a young man for whom lynching and rape are the law and order of the day whining about political correctness. This is a woman trying (and failing) to talk the young man out of his own murderous madness. As people will do, Rufus derisively waves away the living fact of the history he's sitting in and perpetuating.

Sounds familiar. What is political correctness if not the pressure of realities that call me outside of my own mental comfort zone, my own feverish feed of self-legitimation? Give me a word like *bias*, and I can rationalize away every fact, every honest word anyone attempts in my presence, the lived experience of millions of people, to my own lonely and defensive satisfaction.

How do we not do this? By being people of liberating artfulness. By doing daily battle with our own ignorance and, as often as possible, the ignorance of others. As philosopher-poets, we get to practice deep wit, deep skepticism, and deep care when it comes to the words we speak and consider, the stories we take in and tell. We get to watch our language.

Are you what you would call progressive? Wonderful. Define what you take to be progress and what you're willing to do to see it through. Conservative?

That's quite a task to take on. Name some things you wish to conserve. What do we have in mind when we cling to words like these? What do we hope for? What do we fear?

If we're going to use these labels on ourselves or others, we'll need to be really clear about what we mean and don't mean. In a community of thoughtfulness, our job is to be as real as we can with the language we have. Others (Prince, Emily Dickinson, Ralph Waldo Emerson) have gone before us. The awareness campaign we get to undertake together as writers and readers, listeners and thinkers, has long been underway, beckoning us in, for centuries. Tradition, G. K. Chesterton once asserted, is just the democracy of the dead.[12] Books are people talking. What we call literature is nothing more nor less than the greatest hits of the human species. The ancient work of recognition is never done, and anyone with an ear to hear or a mind to pick up what's been laid down is invited to join in. Self-examination, I try to assert in the classroom and beyond, is what makes a beautiful life possible. And an unexamined playlist is not worth having.

We Demonize When We Don't Know What to Do with Our Despair

The morning of November 9, 2016, the forces of unexamination, by most accounts, decisively won the day.

Other than reading aloud William Stafford's "A Ritual to Read to Each Other,"[13] I didn't know where to begin. For many of my students, it was as if the bottom had dropped out of their emotional lives, as if the crazy tyrant hate clown of *Mad Max: Fury Road* was riding into the White House on a wave of mutilation. One student told me she had to listen to podcasts all day to deal with the fact that her parents were celebrating. It was like they couldn't be made to see that they'd peed in her drinking water. Another who's serving a life sentence darkly joked that she feels safer in prison.

For almost every student who'd communicated support for Donald Trump, there were students who let me know they required a day or two to prepare themselves before they'd feel comfortable sitting in the same room with his supporters again. But down to a person, if they didn't look alarmed over the prospect of a Trump presidency, they looked frightened by how frightened their peers were over something that was only beginning to sound like a big deal. Everyone was freaked out.

After I read my Stafford poem and established a few ground rules (no demonizing, no cutting anyone off), I tried to hang back. I imagine any class that involves me talking more than half of the time is a class that's probably gone very badly, and I managed to keep quiet that day.

We agreed that we didn't know for sure what we were in for yet and that we'd have to wait to see which of Trump's threats were bluffs, which of his promises were jokes. No one appeared to hold out hope that he would one day genuinely apologize for his boasts of sexual assault or his call for the execution of innocent black men or that he would ever actually read the document he would soon swear to preserve, protect, and defend.

As we discussed the amount of trust our system was about to hand over to a man none of us would feel completely comfortable leaving alone with a child, we began to voice fears for ourselves, our families, and all the people Trump targeted—that would be most people—as his alleged enemies. When a couple of students tried to dismiss these fears as unfounded, implying that such sentiments were the product of hysteria, I was inspired to see the majority gently focus the exchange toward firm resolutions in response: no one gets to explain away another person's experience. And more importantly: you don't get to feel offended by someone else's bodily fear. You get to listen to them.

We demonize people when we feel powerless. We demonize when we don't know what to do with our own despair. But mad, we noted, is ever a form of sad, and our channels for engaging despair thoughtfully can't be controlled by nor are they dependent upon any elected official. We can make our own moments of pause together with others whenever we like. We resolved not to let the more-than-daily outbursts of that most famously insecure man dictate our emotional lives or the way we would address one another. Trump's mental chaos, his best-selling toxic understanding of himself and others, need not, we noted, become our own because we get to choose what we take in. And as we have to do with anyone who would try to reduce the whole world to the size of their own fear, we can respond with thoughtfulness at every turn. We can make of our own speech, our actions, and our thinking a neighborhood expression of care.

Psychic Blast of Blessedness

I borrow this phrase—neighborhood expression of care—from video footage of what I take to be an exemplary instance of soft exorcism, a model for the kind of exchange that, though hardly ever publicized, probably overcomes estrangement, de-escalating tensions, thousands of times a day. It's the testimony of that beautiful adult Fred Rogers, given before the Senate Subcommittee on Communications chaired by Senator John Pastore. In the video, Rogers offers a philosophical argument for the funding of public television and his own labor of love, *Mister Rogers'*

Neighborhood, which Pastore—this is 1969—knows nothing about.[14]

Slowly and steadily and while maintaining constant eye contact, Rogers asks permission to go off script. He speaks of trust, his own deep confidence that the senator, like others in the room, shares his concerns for the emotional lives of American children, and the inner drama of the child. He then wonders if the senator might agree with him as he almost reluctantly characterizes much of the popular children's television programming as a form of "bombardment." He wonders: Why not do it differently? Is a slower and more imaginative engagement that prioritizes a child's needs worthy of public funding? Will it promote the general welfare?[15]

From there, he describes his own lifelong effort to speak to human anxiety constructively. For Rogers, it involves puppets, music, and listening closely to children, his neighborhood expression of care. His bottom line? To "make it clear that feelings are mentionable and manageable," and to cultivate, with and for the neighbors that are his viewers, the good feeling of self-control available to each of us whenever we're confronted with perceived conflict, whenever we're rattled, whenever we're afraid we might lose it.[16] Needless to say, Rogers practices his bottom line right then and there with every grown child present.

And just as the goose-bumps level, by Senator Pastore's own testimony, looks to have maxed out, Rogers asks if he might recite a song whose title is the question of the hour (maybe every hour): "What Do You Do with the Mad That You Feel?" It's as if he's treated everyone present to a psychic blast of blessedness. Rogers pauses to note that the question was purloined from a child struggling with this very issue aloud.[17]

We each have the power to stop, stop, stop, Rogers instructs, as he gently strikes the table, when we've planned something, in word or action, that will go badly for ourselves and others. There is something deep within us—an inner resource, our intuition, our core—that can come to our aid when we need it most. Our feelings, we can access the realization at any moment, are mentionable and manageable. We can know and experience "that good feeling of control."[18] We can become what we're supposed to be.

Needless to say, Fred Rogers got his (and our) funding. The power he channeled, as paradoxical as it sounds, was the strongest voice in the room. He spoke as one with real authority, the authority of a real and loving person, a good neighbor.

With most of my classes during the presidential election of 2016, I watched this marvel of a video. And we reached a general consensus that "What do you do with the mad that you feel?" is probably the kind of question we'd do well to put to anyone seeking public office. We should also put the question to ourselves as often as possible, answering it as honestly as we can when we do. It's the question of our own reactivity, which is, of course, mirrored in the larger world. There is no effective facing down of dark forces *out there* till we face down the dark forces within. When we avoid this kind of self-examination, we strengthen, each in our own way, the movement of denialism that often seizes the levers of ultimate power in palaces, board rooms, and offices in Washington, DC, and across the country.

We can differ in our views of what true neighborliness consists of, but we can't rightly leave the question of neighborliness behind in anything we're up to. We're enjoined by the creative labor of those who precede us to find language to match our feelings and fears and to somehow do justice to what's going on. Marvin Gaye's *What's Going On* is a neighborhood expression of care. Adrienne Rich's "Diving into the Wreck" is a neighborhood expression of care. A sit-in is a neighborhood expression of care. An anti-racist book club too. There have been so many. They're all around us, even now. Artifacts and actions of poetic responsiveness— of moral seriousness—are everywhere. We get to make more, together with others, in the face of despair. One breath at a time.

As we try to stay sane and see clearly while responding to the fact of the insurrection of January 6, the Big Lie, the forced-birth movement, and the ascendance of Christofascism, we'll need to draw on our inner resources and the neighborly expressions of others constantly. The reigning toxicity of denialism is upon us, but we have the resources, inner and outer, to bring renewed thoughtfulness to our every exchange, even when our attempts at thoughtfulness are met with more denial.

There Are Always Words to Be Had

As I search my own mind, grasping for models of resistance, I draw strength from a scene recounted in Congressman John Lewis's March trilogy when five-hundred-plus activists preparing to march to demonstrate for the right to vote were confronted by Alabama state troopers on the Edmund Pettus Bridge in Selma on Bloody Sunday, March 7, 1965. As these heroic Americans prepared themselves for the tear gas and the beatings to come, an exchange occurred. With state troopers under his command, Major John Cloud gave the order to disperse: "This is an unlawful assembly. Your march is not conducive to the public safety. You are ordered to disperse and go back to your church or to your homes."

Standing at the forefront of the marchers gathered on the bridge, Reverend Hosea Williams wondered aloud if Major Cloud might be talked out of the state-sanctioned wickedness he was about to order: "May we have a word with the major?"

The response was definitive: "There is no word to be had."[19] The decree came at them with the force of an alternative fact.

The violence that followed, by being televised, changed history, but not to the advantage of white supremacy. There *was* a word to be had, the next day and the day after that and in the decades to come down to our day, our radioactive days. The neighborhood expression of care undertaken in Selma, preceded and followed by countless others (famous and not so famous), is essential still to the meaning of human history, at the center of our cultural canon wherever beloved community is evoked, where there are *always* words to be had.

No political party and no presidential administration can prevent such feats of thoughtfulness whether born of a moment, long strategized, or mostly improvised. There is so much precedent for dealing with human madness, so much righteousness to which we might yet be true in new and surprising ways. So many avenues for dramatically conjuring up, for ourselves and our fellow humans, a vision of what's true and lovely and good.

The adult education afforded us by witnesses like Octavia Butler, Fred Rogers, and John Lewis is amplified by words of counsel from the poet Mary Oliver.

Fittingly, she describes the emotional centering a child requires, which is, of course, also the centering needful for grown-ups at the mercy of other grown-ups here, there, and everywhere: "The child whose gaze is met learns that the world is real, and desirable—that the child himself is real, and cherished."[20] If we're to hold ourselves together, we'll have a lot of gazing to do and much cherishing of those who've been made to feel—and expect to go on feeling—decidedly *un*cherished.

May we each meet one another's gaze—perhaps especially the gazes of those whose words and actions horrify us—as we try to be as real as we can in the dangerous days upon us. As was always the case, we aren't only responsible for our own ideas; we're responsible, too, for the ideas we allow others to lift up unchallenged in our presence. We get to engage our collective anxiety constructively, one neighborhood expression of care at a time. The culture that produced the moral failure of the insurrection era is *our* culture.

> We aren't only responsible for our own ideas; we're responsible, too, for the ideas we allow others to lift up unchallenged in our presence.

It seems to me that if we aren't agitated, we aren't paying attention, but the question remains before us: What do we *do* with our agitation? It will require candor and courage and conscience, but there are many words to be had and even more words to be embodied, maybe even for the first time, from here on out.

3

What Does Apocalypse Want from Me?

The prophetic task of naming what's happening

Alongside William Blake, I believe we become what we behold.[1] We're nourished by the gaze of others, in the most positive and righteous sense, but we're also formed by that upon which we gaze, that to which we give our energy and attention. Or as I put it, we become what we do with our attention.

I borrow this way of putting it from the poet Donovan McAbee: "How we waste our days is how we waste our lives."[2]

I love the way this line puts the question of energy expenditure in play. One wild and precious life coming down to how we decide to waste another year after year. Waste management. Time management. It's all relative. Relative to context, I mean. Who's to say what was and wasn't wasteful? Whose time was used well? Who am I to say?

I get a lot of good work done while sleeping, for instance. Sleep is where my conscience (or God) catches up with me, and my dreams begin to show me what I'm doing with my bandwidth and my breakdowns. Which is what I will have done with my life. We emit what we admit.

Let's review. Is this thing on?

Rush Limbaugh once had me at hello, which is to say, he used to take up entirely too much space within my bandwidth, but I eventually, with a lot of help, ceded more of my headspace to others. There is still an awful lot that occupies my bandwidth in less than healthy ways, a lot by which I am not helpfully consumed, but I'm working on it. Again, with more than a little help from my friends. I am formed by my relationships. Peer pressure is forever.

We become what we behold. Ever hear yourself using words you once overheard and have now incorporated into your own thought life so deeply that you've practically forgotten your sources? It's how language and even eloquence—always borrowed, after all—work. The voices we use—or think we use—kinda sorta become our voice.

We become what we voice. It's easy to find our-selves parroting and even believing ideas that, once upon a time, we would have found off-putting. Do we become what we amplify? Do we *become* what we platform? Is psychological continuity possible?

Witness Has No Off Switch

"We don't have a say in his views. We are just a mechanism for his delivery."[3] That's website devel-oper Brad Parscale, referring to his own role in driving home the views of his client, Donald Trump. I'm struck by the distancing operation attempted with the words "say," "mechanism," and "delivery." I understand the impulse to attempt an air of critical detachment when it comes to certain partnerships and associations, but it's not sustainable. The firewall he proposes between himself and his client is illusory. If I publicly repeat the public claim of an abusive pundit, politician, or media personality, am *I* a mechanism for *their* delivery?

I suspect I often am. I risk participating in the pro-liferation of a lie by bringing it to the attention of oth-ers. I might publicly reference the lie for the purpose of publicly differing with it, but I'm still spreading the words, the footage, and/or the screen matter. I'm giv-ing the bully, the autocrat, or the bad faith actor my own energy. *I'm* pushing *their* product and thereby playing the role of content mule. Do I *become* that to which I give oxygen, energy, and the figurative microphone?

I do. There's a deep psychic sense in which we *become* the content we mediate for others. Perhaps especially when we do it in exchange for money. Witness has no off switch. Spirit knows no division.

I can't quite say the thing I said or did or amplified or helped along isn't me. Our anima (our movement, our soul) is involved and implicated. We're adding, giving, slowing, stopping, and checking momentum. Our own momentum and the momentum of others. We play host to the current of people's content. We traffic in the mix of other people's moves and our own. We become what we voice.

Our "likes," our shares, and our decision to hop on a social media platform to weigh in all matter. We can't not matter. We're voting. We're cultivating. We're host-bodying. Our psychological continuity is, after all, in play. We're deciding. Our deciding creates culture. Not sometimes. Always.

Kurt Vonnegut, you'll recall, says we are what we pretend to be and advises us, then, to be very careful what we pretend to be. All this to say we *also* become what we do with our technology (or tools). All media is social. That which we call "social media" is like paper and pen except quicker and easier to reproduce. There are psychic perils, threats to public safety, as well as profound possibilities here.

In our days of easy access to the words and images of others and instantaneous powers of self-publication possessed by anyone with internet access and, for instance, a social media account, having a quick look at an activated screen can feel like trying to keep your wits about you while staring into the spray of a broken fire hydrant. We don't always know how to take it, this horde of human expression coming at us all at once. What does it all mean? Who's to say? And how do you determine the context of something that often comes as a snippet?

Context is hard, but it isn't *that* hard. We can stop at any time. We can slow the hell down. We can, at least for now, give ourselves a break from the false covenant of fake intimacy the magic ring of internet access affords us. Our feelings (deep breath) are mentionable and manageable. Given the stakes, we sometimes need to step back. To maintain psychological continuity—a surviving sense of self—alongside (or despite) "our fully public-data-harvested-known selves" (Jeanette Winterson's phrase),[4] often we'd do well to avoid social media apps like the plague.

As of this writing, I do not, in fact, avoid social media like the plague. Truth be told, I am often "on" it. It (or, rather, the quick, remote access to interactive content it promises) pulls me in like a siren song. I relish the ease of getting into it with people with the aid of a screen and the push of a button, and, alas,

I enjoy the too-easy escape into . . . well, it's hard to say where exactly.

If you do hop on, it's catastrophically easy to misunderstand the assignment. It's easy to look into the black mirror, forget where you are, and feel like you're drowning in a sea of reactivity, a psychic showroom that accelerates your capacity to feel foolish and speak foolishly. If you're like me, you believe and suspect and feel intensely all kinds of things. Feelings become thoughts become a swarm of opinions. If you're like me, some of your opinions aren't as well examined as others. Might the internet afford us a space for examination and inquiry?

Here again, like printed material, the screen can be a tool in undertaking the essential and, to my mind, holy work of examining our own opinions in light of incoming data, of trying to become someone upon whom nothing is lost, someone who doesn't settle for or succumb to unexamined opinions. Unexamined opinions have a way of becoming unexamined decisions, which have a way of becoming unexamined policies. To not slow down, check myself, or poke around to research whether or not what I'm saying, sharing, and getting worked up over is true is to be the target market, the easy prey, of disinformation culture. Long before smartphones, it was observed that *that* life, the unexamined life, is not worth living.[5]

"People are saying . . ." the saying goes. "Studies have shown . . ." "It says here that . . ." But the prophet side of my heart, like Patti Smith, is called to inquire further. Who said it exactly? What's the context? Who paid for the so-called studies? Where we stand determines what we say and see.

The Voice of Honest Indignation

Reaction is easy and inevitable. Response is slower and made possible by careful analysis and receptivity as I scroll and see and process and scroll some more. An app can amplify my capacity for the demonic. It can amplify my capacity for the poetic and the prophetic too.

And to speak or act or see prophetically is to acknowledge and confront normalized hypocrisies, the moral contradictions that are hidden, the relationships that are purposefully obscured to justify ill-gotten gain. Anyone can do it. Anyone can shine light on unjust systems. Anyone can take up the prophetic task. Pen, pencil, camera, canvas, megaphone, cell phone. Let's not confuse the tools for the form. The avenues to artfulness are everywhere.

The prophetic task is to publicly dramatize the moral unseriousness that's otherwise normalized, excused, often masked, and crushingly well-funded. This task is taken up in art, activism, everyday expressions of candor, and even on Twitter. It's a witness I miss if I'm only alert to incoming data that flatters me, data that won't upset me or threaten my posture and privilege. If my heart is defensive or easily offended, the prophetic is often lost on me.

To keep my third eye open lest I mistake an emotional reaction for a meaningful response, I have a paraphrase purloined from William Blake for thinking through words or images that might initially trigger me: the voice of honest indignation is the voice of God.[6] Slow the tape and mull that one over a little: the voice of honest indignation is the voice of God. This doesn't mean any and everyone's frustrations can be helpfully decreed a form of sacred writ, but it *does* mean I must take very seriously every honest word that comes from me or at me, even if someone's word choice might initially offend.

Blake knew something about the doors of perception. The job is to be alert and open to transformation. Is there information to be had in the fact of what offends me and doesn't? Oh my, yes. Might someone else's expression of very legitimate anger be a source of moral revelation—an apocalypse, even—that demands something of me? Yes, and more yes. The voice that comes to trouble me is more than likely my own.

Many lurkers and practitioners scrolling through Twitter on August 26, 2020, likely happened upon these words: "FUCK THIS MAN!!!! WE DEMAND CHANGE. SICK OF IT."[7] No context was provided, and, if you were among the already tuned-in, none was required.[8] This was LeBron James. We know his tone, and we know his love and his bodily commitment to the safety and thriving of Black people. King James was voicing an anguished public reaction to the latest disclosure, the catastrophic clockwork, of more white supremacist terror footage. As Jacob Blake tried to enter an SUV, with his three sons in the back seat, Officer Rusten Sheskey of Kenosha, Wisconsin, shot him in the back seven times. Handcuffed to his hospital bed, he was left paralyzed from the waist down.[9] As of this writing, Officer Sheskey remains on the police force and was never subjected to discipline.[10]

With over fifty-two million followers and counting,[11] James's online transmission struck a chord. How does one measure questions of impact, solidarity, and civility when thinking through the meaning of such gestures? Was King James out of line? Did this just add to the noise?

Consider this: the power to forcibly decree what is or isn't civility is quite the power. It's right up there with the power to forcibly decree what is or isn't normal. On or off Twitter, the data is incoming. What we do or don't do with what we know, what we come to realize, is on us. Which terrors will we allow within our bandwidth? Which aggressions will go unchecked?

Decisions, on the global and granular level, add up and cascade into cultures.

King James made a choice regarding his globally formidable brand, his own power of witness as a mandated reporter having seen what he saw, and the available levers of an app called Twitter.

One could stop there with a philanthropist athlete's online signal flare, bristle at the language, mimic the popular line that he should stick to basketball, and scroll on. But to do so would be to refuse the prophetic and miss an apocalypse—the eye-opener—the invitation to look longer, see further, and *feel more*. To front at the sight of it, as if King James were the one behaving inappropriately, would be to deny oneself deeper recognition of King James's longer, more righteous game.

By clicking Tweet, James was strategically contributing to the gathering momentum of civic courage within which the Milwaukee Bucks boycotted Game 5 of the NBA playoffs and WNBA players wore shirts that collectively spelled out Jacob Blake's name on the front and had seven bullet holes printed on the back.[12] Courage is contagious. Group courage has a way of meeting one apocalypse with another one. Prophets make the most of every available apocalypse, personal and public.

The summer of 2020 was full of famous and unfamous people taking up the prophetic task. Did you notice?

Unchecked terror holds sway until it's checked. We become what we abide. King James declined to sit this one out. By choosing to take up the prophetic task, he also set a table for the public expression of dismay, despair, and discernment within the professional sports community. Public grief and candor, in the hours that followed, were the norm. King James's spirited decision undertaken, I presume, on his smartphone, was a spark that got a righteous fire going. His broadcast, via tweet, set a more open scene of free expression, a broader horizon of expectation beyond the wide world of sports. To consider social media is to consider the potentiality of such prophetic catalysts, the question of what will or won't or might yet move the needle.

Within hours the Clippers's coach, Doc Rivers, saw fit to publicly comment upon the kind of rhetoric coming out of the Republican National Convention of 2020. He noted that, among supporters of the Trump administration, he kept hearing about fear. Weaponized despair and for-profit rancor were, it's well understood, both the product Republicans were selling *and* the mechanism for delivery, but Rivers had a larger point to make in view of events in Kenosha.

The hate mongers' insistent overplaying of their own hand whenever news of police brutality surfaces beggars belief. The stoking of anxiety by white people over what *might* happen if law enforcement is made morally accountable, Rivers argued, is a cruel circus: "*We're* the ones getting killed. . . . *We've* been hung. *We've* been shot. . . . It's amazing to me . . . why we keep loving this country, and this country *does not* love us back."[13]

In conversation with Ari Melber, sports columnist, William C. Rhoden described the state of play entering a new phase of call-and-response, where unchecked moves make for unchecked momentum until someone risks a move to place the check. Now and then and always, one move invites another. Rhoden honed in on Officer Sheskey's terror enacted upon Jacob Blake but also widened the frame.

As Rhoden sees it, "It's almost as if it's a dare." As "state-sponsored violence" escalates in one city after another, professional athletes are challenged anew. "What are you gonna do now? What are you gonna do next? . . . It's not really complicated. It's emotional, but it's not that complicated."[14]

King James had occasion to process aloud his reaction to the footage of Jacob Blake being shot. A word after a word after a word is power, Margaret Atwood tells us.[15] King James helped push and hold open a door earlier in the day and now stepped into the space he conjured together with others to offer more words: "If you're sitting here and telling me there was no way to subdue that gentleman or detain him . . . before the firing of guns—then you're sitting here, and you're lying to not only me, you're lying to . . . every African American, every Black person in the community."[16] The moral imperative now, James would later put it, is "to keep our foot on the gas,"[17] to keep the discourse going. There's a time to slow your roll. But not now.

It wasn't over. This insistence on staying focused and maintaining a momentum of awareness and resistance continued to resonate. This was evident on August 27 when the New York Mets and the Miami Marlins took to the field, observed forty-two seconds of silence to commemorate Jackie Robinson, and then walked off the field, declining to play, and leaving behind a Black Lives Matter shirt draped over home plate.[18] The needle was moving.

The next day, the Ole Miss football team walked out on practice to protest police brutality and commemorate the sixty-fifth anniversary of Emmett Till's murder,[19] and the NBA announced its intention to turn stadiums across the country into voting locations to allow for social distancing on Election Day.[20] Consider the cascade of action and awareness King James and his moral partners within our nation's sports community put into effect.

Here again, association is currency. The invitation to take up the prophetic task is open to all comers, the people of the commons and popular icons alike. There's a democratic dignity at work in popular culture because the boundaries between content, creators, and the audience often prove porous. Pop cult is comprised of subcults that constantly jump the presumed barricades of politics, public safety, art, sports, and entertainment. To divide them up at all is to let marketing strategists do our thinking for us. Unexamined thinking yields unexamined policies that get people shot, killed, tortured, and caged. When it's righteous, popular culture eats ugly policy for breakfast. Honest indignation, the voice of God—if we let it—hastens the lived realization of incoming data.

If honest indignation is a form of sacred expression, a curse can be rightly thought of as prayer and prophecy, calling for situational awareness concerning the terror and trauma we harmfully abide, shining a light on what remains harmfully hidden. Perhaps King James's profanity prayer is being answered. Do we hear it?

Where we stand determines what we see. As a white southerner in America, I have a holy obligation to receive and consider the signals of people of color whose experiences differ from my own, to fight easy ignorance posing a terror threat to their lives for centuries. I don't get to think of King James's cry of anguish (or anyone's cries of anguish) as a needlessly offensive disturbance of my peace. To be a morally responsive person is to be awakened by that witness and to process and respond.

To Not Disgrace Oneself

If I refuse to be moved by prophetic utterance, that refusal can't be blamed on the internet or Twitter or "social media." That refusal is on me. This is where fastidiousness is often a form of privilege. This is also where terror and prurience lock arms against data that unsettles the abusers' status quo.

I don't have King James's cash flow, but I know feelingly that my life isn't in danger the way his is even now. Prophecy pays a price. But will I let *my* context be informed by *his*? Will I register the gift of spirit he held out via tweet? If I won't, that's a dis-grace.

Disgrace is something of a hot-button word within reactivity-driven, horse-race media product. The oppositional energy it conjures is doubtless a kind of ratings gold. If we slow the tape enough, though, the verb/noun can prove helpful. To be alert to the subtleties in the operation of disgrace is essential to the prophetic tasks before us. Is this thing on? Consider the two syllables that form the word *disgrace*.

There's the biological fact of beloved community, relatedness and kinship, the common heart of things. As Shakespeare tells us, "One touch of nature makes the whole world kin."[21] This, to me, is grace. It's everywhere and all around us.

And then there are moves, behaviors, speech, and even policies that amount to forms of *dis*grace.

To act disgracefully is to act against what's natural and good. If you're like me, you don't often realize you're acting disgracefully while you're in the thick of it. It's usually only later, having slowed my roll a little, that I see reactivity got the best of me and register the damage I've done. Probably when I felt cornered and afraid. Or when I felt the hot breath of peer pressure. Even then, with compassion, curiosity, and the wise counsel of others, I can recognize when I've behaved disgracefully.

To publicly decree a person—my fellow creature, after all—a disgrace is to attempt to otherize them completely and definitively. "Disgrace," the smear, is often reactively applied to anyone who interrupts my morally flattering fantasies. When I think or speak of another person *as* a disgrace, I disgrace myself. Maybe that's how disgrace works. Perhaps one can only disgrace oneself. But one can harm communities and kinship beyond the self.

As LeBron James and other individuals (famous and unfamous) came to recognize their own moral power in new ways during the summer marked by the murder of George Floyd, many disgraced themselves by seeking to belittle, bully, and marginalize the prophetic witness by calling it polarizing, partisan, and needlessly "political." As I see it, we're still catching up to the collective apocalypse of that summer (preceded by the related apocalypse of the dawn of the COVID-19 era).

There is nothing disgraceful about deciding you'd rather risk your position and lose money than enable white supremacist terror one second longer. That's baseline moral seriousness. It is sometimes contagious. Here and there, and certainly in the wide world of sports, the work of *not* disgracing oneself by remaining silent in the presence of crushingly wicked deeds is never done.

The Myth of Critical Detachment

Claudia Rankine has an essential adage for the prophetic work of bearing creative witness—to what we see and know and experience—and letting the chips fall: "If you don't name what's happening, everyone can pretend it's not happening."[22]

There's an urgency here too easily glossed over by people who, like myself, are armed to the teeth with privilege and long conditioned to silently play along with disgraceful arrangements normalized through moral inertia and the bystander effect. Apocalypse punctures our pretense, our appeals to plausible deniability, and our sense of learned helplessness. Apocalypse invites us to gather our wits and name the problem poetically, prophetically, and properly.

Apocalypse is personal *and* political because it unmasks the myth of critical detachment as an ugly farce. We're made to see that our skin is already in the game. Time to start acting like it.

There are doubtless times when it's healthy and helpful to conceive oneself as someone around whom things randomly happen. Lightning strikes. Accidents will indeed happen. But there are other times when accepting that self-conception means I've succumbed to a kind of moral cowardice and am on the verge of disgracing and debasing myself. Being at all acquainted with my own moral power means knowing the difference and acting upon this knowledge.

Understanding the human assignment means reading the room, registering my context, and discerning the spirits of the times—figuring out what's needful and what I might see that others don't, what my responsibilities are.

If the appeal to spirits sounds like a scriptural reference, it is.[23] I teach (or try to teach) general education classes as well as world religions, religion and science fiction, and, most spring semesters, understanding the Bible. I try to encourage my classes to think of authors of the biblical collection as contemporaries confronted by many of the same challenges and buoyed by many of the same hopes we're awash in today.

In the semesters preceding 2020, I worried that my Bible class was too much of a monologue in which I mused aloud and a few students helped me along with affirming nods. Too few questions peppered the room. Trying to provoke them into disagreeing with

Jesus or Isaiah aloud was all too often a quiet affair. "What does all that have to do with right now?" was a question I'd raise though often found myself trying to answer all by my lonesome.

COVID-19 flipped the script. In 2020, having started out in-person, we returned from spring break entirely remote. The questions came at me with an unprecedented urgency and fierceness. The Bible and the always-open question of what it *says* was alive and signaling across the country. One question arising in our online back-and-forth saw us through to the end of the semester and picked up again in the semesters that followed: Is this the end of the world?

There are two concepts we'd covered (or tried to cover already) that came to our aid in thinking this one through. *The day of the Lord* is both one big day on which, it is alleged, God will make everything right (the last will be first and the first will be last, oppression will cease, people will get what they need to live, the reign of God will come on earth as it already is in heaven) *and* most any day when something like this happens for any group of people anywhere in the world.

The day of the Lord is promised for real. It's also a righteously mobile metaphor. Israelites being led out of slavery in Egypt was a day of the Lord, as was the Emancipation Proclamation and the day people of color got to vote in South Africa and Jewish people being released from concentration camps *and*, for morally serious people everywhere, the legalization of same-sex marriage in America. Here again, where we stand determines what we see. What the day of the Lord means to us will depend on our perceived necessities, our contexts, our actual values, and what we really think of as righteousness.

The other big concept we talked about in class, one the Bible gives us for thinking about the end of the world, is *apocalypse*, which simply means unveiling. An apocalypse occurs when we're suddenly made to see what's going on (in a field, in an emergency room, on my phone, in a car, in therapy, or over coffee). Apocalypse opens our eyes.

In the spring of 2020, our class knew feelingly that we were in the thick of one. Apocalypse had had our attention since we last saw one another. Like most of us and to my shame, before COVID-19, I didn't really live with an awareness that my fellow human beings who work at Amazon / Whole Foods, Kroger, McDonalds, Walmart, didn't get paid sick leave. COVID-19 hit and . . . I found I was thinking about it all the time. I was ready to riot. Moral rot once hidden to me was now plain as day. An apocalypse had occurred. A feeling of urgency concerning my fellow creatures set in as the myth of critical detachment was overcome. To avoid disgracing myself further, I'll need to steward it and live as a newly aware person, bearing fruit in keeping with my apocalypse.

And in the case of Kroger, so many of us realized it and didn't like it and said something and then . . . behold, CEO Rodney McMullen changed the policy. This, too, is an apocalypse, a really great one in fact. Deeper realizations of our own connectedness have resulted in deeper practices of neighborly love among essential workers, customers, and employers. Apocalypse can do that. In an apocalypse, relationships that were hidden come to light and—voila—the order of things changes, and it starts with our demanding it has to change.

Empires Will Empire

In time, Starbucks stores around the country would successfully unionize. Amazon labor organizer Christian Smalls would not get a hearing in the bodily presence of Jeff Bezos, but he would secure a meeting with President Joe Biden. Apocalypses have a way of adding up. And sometimes rail strikes show how unions are still strong-armed by the strong. But apocalypse once begun begets apocalypse.

The Great Economy, that's what Wendell Berry calls the kingdom of God imagined and sought after by Jesus and other prophets.[24] We can also call it the Deep Economy or God's Economy or True Economy. We might also call it, in Neil Peart's phrase, the Real Relation, which can be discerned as an "underlying theme,"[25] though often obscured, in human consciousness. The Great Economy is that which makes all economies possible.

Eco in Greek is *oikos*, which means "house." The Great Economy is a way of naming the great unknown (which is most of what is). The house that houses all (including all that is arguably unhoused).

The American economy, as it is currently arranged, *is not* that kind of economy. But, thanks to the apocalypse that is and was and will have been our pandemic, many of us who were in the grip of particular fantasies about ourselves and others have been made to consider the pain of this arrangement—the American arrangement—and to see anew what it costs us and the neighbors we learned, for a time, to speak of as "essential workers." Apocalypse has a beautiful way of making us more alive to questions of essence. If we're alert to it, apocalypse can turn our thinking around, restore our senses, and save our souls. Within an apocalypse, our sense of detachment doesn't stand a chance. The question of economy, whether suddenly or slowly, becomes the question of what's truly essential.

If we substitute that definitive-feeling word *economy* with the word *arrangement* (which is what an economy is), new possibilities begin to unfold. And positively, we see that the arrangement we've settled for and *agreed to* isn't true or just or balanced or beautiful enough. It's in danger of collapsing in on itself, and many of us know, in our hearts, that it didn't have to be this way. The collapse of wicked arrangements, after all, are well deserved and righteously longed for. In the language of scripture, this "Lord, come quickly" ask is a call for the speeding of the collapse.

So . . . is it the end of one world? Certainly. It often is. But there might be a better one around the bend, a better arrangement (economy) than the one we've normalized. Maybe there's a more righteous order (new and old) on the way. The question is: Will we agree to it?

Are we on the side of the billionaire pharaohs who want to accrue more wealth while endangering the mental and physical health of people who make their own lives possible with their labor? Do we want the people who prepare, stock, and deliver our goods to have access to safety, general welfare, to life and livelihood? The ancient world was attuned to such changes, and sacred scripture emerged out of their lively, self-effacing, and sometimes faithful obedience to the apocalypse in their midst.

Egypt, Babylon, and Rome tried to impose their so-called orders on the human form divine, and these communities watched and foresaw their collapse. We are undoubtedly seeing such things occur in our day too. And yet our everyday collapse is sometimes also an apocalypse, an everyday kind, if we let it be. "Empires will empire" as Brittany Paschall once put it.[26] But an apocalypse will also apocalypse.

One Thing Has to Do with Another

An economy is an arrangement, but it also may be considered an *agreement*. We become what we agree to. We can speak of values and virtues as sacred things we carry around in our hearts, but our values are only ever what we execute and embody in our getting, spending, and speaking. And our perceived virtues—our values—as much as we like to tout them, have nowhere else to happen but here.

> We can speak of values and virtues as sacred things we carry around in our hearts, but our values are only ever what we execute and embody in our getting, spending, and speaking.

Apocalypse—the great eye-opener—shows us what we've agreed to, what our perceived have-to's (our perceived necessities) are, and affords us the opportunity to think it all through again, to turn the mind around in such a way that our behaviors follow along.

And if an economy isn't nimble enough to bend in the direction of equal access among its sustainers, access to what we each need to live and thrive, it needs to be replaced, which can be conceived, less dramatically, as rearrangement. Our arrangements hold until they don't. The creative, moral mindset that informs the prophetic task here would have us see that the "days of the Lord" are many and our apocalypses (like the arrangements they challenge) are interlocking.

Behold, again, the intersections! Yes, they're overwhelming. Especially when we've only recently been made to see that they're there. But one thing having to do with another (every fact is a function of relationship) isn't a disaster. It simply is. Intersections are everywhere. Literal and figurative. Within and without. An apocalypse makes the intersections of all our arrangements once obscured more plain. Time to say what we're seeing. If we don't *say* what's happening, we can pretend it isn't. The prophetic task is to stop pretending.

Intersectionality, meanwhile, means noticing— and insisting—that one thing has to do with another. Before it appeared among us as a legal term the bigoted want to ban, intersectionality existed among us as the fact of relationship. To imagine poetically, think critically, and act prophetically is to lean into the realization of relationship instead of denying or fleeing it. This will call for specificity and, if you're like me, committing to a public recognition of some unflattering data.

To get at the intersections, it is sometimes necessary to speak of spirit, which, we understand, defies boundaries, divisions, and compartmentalized thinking. Do you sense spirits sometimes? I do. Poltergeists too.

4

White Supremacist Antichrist Poltergeist

Discerning a spirit

When I'm quiet and managing to breathe in a more conscious way than usual, unflattering memories sometimes come to me in a rush.

My reactive self often views unflattering memories as an existential threat, an attack on my identity and therefore my core, my very being. When an unflattering memory is on the verge of surfacing, my reactive self goes nuts. It's a little ugly. Apocalypse.

Cue my responsive self, which is capable of considering and contemplating unflattering memories. At my best, I can even welcome them because they help me receive the sense that I am a part of that which scares and upsets me, that which I'm all too prone to try to distance myself from. I, too, have made a stranger of myself. I, too, have succumbed to the behaviors I see among bad faith actors who pose a threat to themselves and others, who belittle their fellow creatures to accrue cred and coin. Here comes the unflattering memory:

I was nineteen years old when I went to see Spike Lee's 1989 film *Do the Right Thing* at Vanderbilt University's Sarratt Cinema. This screening included a panel discussion with Joie Lee and Giancarlo Esposito, who appear in the film.

I was shaken by it. At fifty-three, I'm still trying to face the facts of it, to pick up more of what Spike Lee and his creative team show with this film. It remains an education. A gift of an apocalypse that keeps right on giving. The unflattering memory begins with the discussion that followed.

I was one of very few white people in attendance. Giancarlo Esposito remarked that he was pleased to see so many sisters and brothers in the audience and expressed his longing and desire for more sisters and brothers in the creative arts and the film industry in particular. I'm ashamed to say this didn't land well with me. Fear bit me: a triggered and defensive feeling arose within me. A question began to form in my mind: *Am I a brother?*

I also imagined a follow-up: *If not, why not?*

I did not ask these questions. But I imagined asking them. Imagined that if I asked them I would have everyone's attention and they would perceive me as clever. That energy made me feel strong on the drive home as I worked to not examine the feeling arising in me. Unexamined feelings have a way of adding up, cascading into unexamined grievances—or *perceived* grievances—that, when nourished, transmogrify into actual enmity and contempt. Reader, it gets worse.

A fantasy began to take hold. In the days and weeks that followed, I started recounting aloud, in front of people, what Giancarlo Esposito said about sisters and brothers that night and the questions I'd thought of but hadn't asked. More than a few white people seemed to agree that these were good and important questions that someone should have asked. In time, it became an anecdote I shared in certain circles to endear myself to (white) others.

It became one of my bits for a time, a rhetorical flex with a particular demographic. But, as you might guess, it wasn't a story I told to Black colleagues or in front of Black people. Doing so would have risked something I wasn't interested in risking. The energy I was after did not involve that kind of vulnerability. Male fantasies die hard. White male fantasies die harder. I wanted mine fed. I craved affirmation and often got it from the crowds I craved it from. I knew how to curate a crowd and get what I was looking for.

To Love a Person Is to Love a Process

Thinking back on it now, I can begin to see how getting affirmed, here and there, for being an idiot, added up for a time. I thank God the internet wasn't available to me in those days. I have clippings as grim reminders of some ugly sentences I set down in high school and college newspapers. My brand has been well-served by the fact that those sentences escaped public scrutiny. If, at the time, I'd been handsomely compensated to be that version of myself in public, my life now would look very different. I was a piece of work.

Unflattering, harmful, harming. Those shame-filled memories, like little apocalypses that catch up to us, can give us the data we need to overcome the defenses and denials that impede ethics, truth, and compassion for unsavory versions of ourselves we'd perhaps like to disavow. Best not to disavow. Better still to own all the parts. Better to *re*member what I'd like to *dis*member. Better to do the work of examining all the parts that are and were the process of who I am.

To love a person is to love a process. That's a line I have on repeat. I'm a process, and so are you. Why not linger in the fact of what I was up to as an anxious nineteen-year-old in the late eighties? Why not see what's on the other side of shame?

At that point in time, while I lived it, I did not have the word *whiteness* available to me. Or rather, I had yet to access it. It's possible that Joie Lee or

Giancarlo Esposito spoke the word that evening. If they did, I didn't even entertain the sound of the word long enough to feel shut down by it. It went right past me. I have words for whiteness now.

Whiteness is a way of not seeing, saying, or listening. A form of group denial thought up, set up, and armed to the teeth for centuries.

Whiteness is an investment in not knowing (or pretending to not know) things and belittling (aloud or internally) anyone within range who questions the perceived soundness of that investment. There's an energy to it. An energy that empties people out. An emptying energy. An unclean spirit *and* a social construct. An idol in the true sense, something worshipped that gets hold of people like an idea we can't let go of without losing a sense of security and ugly belonging. It's an arrangement in which people exchange debasement and estrangement for standing and safety. A cult? You bet. Cults demand sacrifice.

Whiteness plays for keeps. A heady drug, whiteness is subtle as hell and also breathtakingly unsubtle. My memory of the *Do the Right Thing* screening in Nashville is one example in which whiteness was doing my seeing, thinking, and speaking for me, but there are many, many more. I also know that there are similar instances, throughout my life, that have yet to surface and likely won't this side of the flatline. I have zero doubt there are more to come.

Whiteness is a disgrace, a terror within and without. Whiteness is weaponized grievance. Which is to say, whiteness names a form of hell, a catastrophically disordered want arising out of felt need, fear, and a crushingly well-funded marketing scheme. Fortunately, it's been studied.

Fear, Trembling, and Specificity

I do not laugh. I am quite straight-faced as I ask soberly:

"But what on earth is whiteness that one should so desire it?" Then always, somehow, some way, silently but clearly, I am given to understand that whiteness is the ownership of the earth forever and ever, Amen!"[1]

Is this thing on? That's W. E. B. Du Bois addressing us from 1920. I don't have to think hard to see what he's referring to. I feel it in my bones. I also dare to say I've known sometimes a different economy: what it's felt like to try to let go of it.

To let go, repent, and begin to get free of whiteness is to adjust my posture and change my position and relinquish an ideology of purity, prurience, and dominance. Whiteness is an ideology, but it is *of course* also a kind of religion that can be hard to shake off, given—hear this—its material benefits. The

"Amen!" of Du Bois states it. Whiteness connotes bodily devotion to something it considers sacrosanct, a *cult* within and across cultures of whiteness, a constellation of interests and spirits demanding obeisance and the active suppression of empathy, conscience, and kinship in exchange for access to power and resources.

To speak of whiteness this way is to speak of something I'm working to daily divest from. For someone with my appearance and background, this starts with naming, confessing, and remaining alert to it as something that has been swallowed like the blue pill, indeed tricked and controlled me, and will continue to if I'm not attentive to its operations. I have to repent of it to get free of it. Given my past, doing so requires daily apocalypses to help me guard my own sense of self against it.

Here again, Thoreau's question, "What demon possessed me that I behaved so well?" helps me think through my silence in the face of injustice when speaking up costs me something. Whiteness is a calculation, an orchestrated silence or sidestepping of conflict, a form of risk aversion that amounts to strategic suppression of my deepest, most imaginative, in-relationship-with-others self. As I seek to educate myself further to repent and get free of these behaviors, I become more aware of all the ways I have yet to be a brother, for to be a brother is to build an economy based in agreement for human thriving, for Black thriving in every form, person, community, and planet.

In Tennessee, that strategic suppression of soul is the price of admission, access, and association in certain contexts. Association, after all, is currency. And in those contexts, the signals are often astoundingly clear. Certain out-loud moral realizations concerning whiteness are an existential threat to the reigning economic arrangements. A feeling, a vibe that bedevils, a demon, a spirit—or a pack of powerful spirits—holds sway and predominates. Here comes the poltergeist.

In the interest of specificity, I'll risk a mouthful of syllables with what I describe as *White Supremacist Antichrist Poltergeist*. In good Christian tradition I'm naming a spirit that gets a hold of people. As a Tennessean who attended a segregation academy for twelve years, I know feelingly that it's had a hold of me.

Calling it a "spirit" helps me name a long economic, systemic line of how this has been handed down, accepted, inhabited, and used, while also acknowledging the truth of that harm with fear, trembling, and specificity of all the ways I've often been complicit in systems that often serve the ends of white supremacist terror. Believing myself blind to it doesn't change the fact of it. White Supremacist Antichrist Poltergeist is not lacking for host bodies.

It surfaces in speech and behavior, toxic reactivity giving way to rage in the harming and killing of Black people daily through police violence, through your and my embrace of power economics.

In an apocalyptic sense, George Floyd Summer brought to the surface what many white people who've operated under the poltergeist's influence never would acknowledge. Idols, literally and figuratively, came down. I was dimly aware, for instance, of a bust of Nathan Bedford Forrest stationed outside the legislative chambers of the Tennessee State Capitol. I'd walked past it as a child. This white supremacist terror idol had been worthy of ridicule my whole life long. Had I thought to ridicule or view it as an assault on human dignity before 2020? I'd never done the research. Yet it was an abomination all along. The young prophets of George Floyd Summer—specifically the "free the plaza" activists who occupied Legislative Plaza, renaming it the Ida B. Wells Plaza—helped me and many of us see this more clearly. Taxpayer-funded abominations are the business of the people. We become what we normalize.

The More We Divide the Less We See

I'll never be able to see that spirit as clearly as my sisters and brothers of color, but I work to be teachable, to educate myself. Thoreau says we all crave reality in one way or another.[2] I think this is true.

How much reality we're willing to acknowledge publicly is another matter entirely. Speaking aloud of White Supremacist Antichrist Poltergeist helps me acknowledge more reality than I'm comfortable acknowledging, but I owe it to myself and others (especially those for whom my militant ignorance is a public safety hazard) to accept the truth of it and act on reality. It's my job as a fellow creature citizen in these United States to try to be more real and therefore more aware. And therefore to act.

The impulse to divide obstructs seeing and speaking clearly. The more we divide the less we see. Whiteness is a spirit I name in hope of expanding the space of the talkaboutable to overcome division. If I can talk about it, I can see it and combat it more effectively. "White Supremacist Antichrist Poltergeist" locates something too few white people name, gives it a label, declares its harm. If I can persuade my fellow whites to say or even entertain the words, many of us might see our way toward repenting and being made more whole.

Whiteness is a poltergeist-sized threat to public safety and mental health. We've been here before. The form of beloved community called church has addressed the challenge it poses across two centuries. In Germany, the Barmen Declaration (1934) addressed the Führer principle as heresy (as well as terror). In South Africa, the Belhar Confession

(1982) addressed white supremacist ideology as sin. And more recently, the Council of Bishops of the African Methodist Episcopal Church issued an Episcopal Statement (2017) that invites "people who are committed to justice and righteousness, equality and truth" to join them in the effort "to thwart what are clearly demonic acts [of the Republican-controlled White House that targeted Muslims, abused asylum seekers, and appointed white supremacist operatives]."[3]

These aren't instances of churches suddenly becoming political. These are instances of communities of baptism showing moral and civic courage, making their witness clear in the face of spiritual threat made manifest in the form of state violence. That's what people of baseline moral seriousness do. There comes a time to name a thing. It matters how we name a thing. Sometimes the name for the thing is antichrist.

With the insertion of *antichrist*, I respond to Du Bois's "Amen!" Whiteness, after all, is often marketed as devout "faith." And, where I come from, it's backed by claims to "biblical authority"—a catastrophically destructive marketing scheme. "Biblical" is a handy-dandy trick used by those who consider themselves devout, belittling and shutting down an opposing view with an unexamined appeal to ancient texts. Among the ironies is this: these ancient texts precede whiteness by centuries. There are no white people in the Bible.

Whiteness Is an Extinction Event

That fact doesn't slow the roll of White Supremacist Antichrist Poltergeist. To be possessed by it is to mistake my whiteness for the Holy Spirit and my claim to power as the exercise of divine right. *Antichrist* is the word for the particular spirit that compels a person to mistake the fear-based drive to power and control for the Christ. It's a word I mean to make the most of. If we don't name what's happening, we can pretend it isn't happening. By naming antichrist within the poltergeist, I'm aiming at the joints and the pressure points of the multipronged myth. I'm aiming at institutions. An institution is a myth with a budget.

White Supremacist Antichrist Poltergeist burns through institutions. It drives a culture of denial in which bad faith operatives find it useful to assert that prayer and the Bible have been outlawed in public schools. That's the fantasy according to which an unrepentant sexual predator holding a Bible in front of church in DC, having tear-gassed nonviolent activists to clear the path, is a show of strength. White Supremacist Antichrist Poltergeist makes brutal appeals to purity, prurience, and dominance to win elections.

This brutal fantasy has a history. Keeping a heart and mind open to a cavalcade of unflattering data, the facts of where we are and where we've been, can feel like a dispiriting task. But now is no time to back down from confronting the evil people like me sometimes ignorantly and sometimes knowingly enabled.

Now is the time to keep going as if the human future depends on it—because it does. The moral summons are being issued everywhere. Whiteness, after all, is an extinction event. As Du Bois assures us, whiteness connotes nothing less than a claim to rightful possession of the humanly inhabitable world. Whiteness also represents the right to destroy it. News product generated by legacy media chasing ad revenue with different sets of words trending at different times brings us: *Christian nationalism*, *MAGA*, and *Trumpists*. But the eye-rubbingly ironic twist is the alighting of White Supremacist Antichrist Poltergeist on an old and beautiful word that got transmogrified into an adjective: *evangelical*.

With breathtakingly thorough analysis, Anthea Butler reveals that the catastrophically powerful voting bloc pollsters refer to as "evangelical" has been commandeered by a network of pundits, politicos, performers, and pastors.[4] Assessing the destruction it has wrought upon our planet requires a clear-eyed and candid consideration of the publicly available history of weaponized whiteness. As someone who once claimed evangelicalism herself, Butler knows the moves, the way the phantom of perceived persecution among powerful, morally unhinged players serves as cover for a verifiably racist agenda. A reckoning, she believes, is underway: "Evangelicals are not being persecuted in America. They are being called to account."[5]

Among the popular icons of evangelicalism over the decades, Butler chronicles missed opportunities as well as racist flexes performed by beloved evangelicals. And Butler invites us to register for real the damage done. Consider this statement from Billy Graham: "*Only* when Christ comes again will little white children of Alabama walk hand in hand with little black children" (emphasis added).[6] Racist poltergeist–spirit sidestepping, shaming, while holding a pious-sounding appeal to Christ alone as the only viable answer to white supremacist terror. In 1963, in response to Martin Luther King Jr.'s "I Have a Dream" speech, this attempted clap back was ugly as hell.

Billy Graham could have recognized King's moral authority and leadership, but instead, what might have been a breakthrough or a public deferral to a fellow pastor's wisdom on racial terror became a defensive move over perceived turf. The vision of Christ espoused by Graham and other high rollers was used over time as a form of "tactical racism," which Butler traces up to our heady present.

It's also worth noting this strategically racist posture is struck within the ideology of Christian supremacy. Graham's response seemingly seeks to edge out the perceived competition. King's ecumenical witness, signaling an interfaith future in which Christianity isn't domineering or dominant, is an existential threat to the white supremacist antichrist poltergeist.

Butler has a phrase for recognizing and holding at a helpful angle the rhetorical strategy whereby racism is passed off as normative by the religious set: "evangelical hostage taking."[7] You might recognize this in moments like Billy Graham's dismissiveness of dream making or the time Jerry Falwell blamed the 9/11 attack on "the gays" and "the ACLU" and Pat Robertson concurred, achieving the desired effect of shutting down inquiry within the evangelical voter bloc.[8]

All That Hell Has to Go Somewhere

In this sense, the operations of White Supremacist Antichrist Poltergeist are subtle but also not at all subtle. A lifetime of white grievance can be overcome but not easily. Here again the prophetic task is clear. Outing it requires exercising our own powers of observation, a determined seeing and saying, again and again, despite all the long-established incentives to ignore it.

This shouldn't be so hard, but deferential fear makes it so for people who cower before and succumb to the poltergeist. I'll return to the language of spirits, but it's also helpful to draw on Charles Mills's read on whiteness as the "Racial Contract" according to which obtuseness (whether hapless, performative, or purposeful) is the price of advancement. This isn't simply fecklessness in the face of injustice. It's "an agreement to misinterpret the world."[9]

Whiteness, in this sense, is a refusal to see, which amounts to a learned incapacity. This requires improvisation. White evangelical operatives and their acolytes are committed and incentivized to actively model the suppression of moral awareness, delivering this product whenever they're on camera. When white people fail, for instance, to rationally process the fact of the January 6 insurrection *as* an insurrection, or fail to process white supremacist gerrymandering in states with a Republican supermajority *as* white supremacist gerrymandering, we demonstrate verifiably that incapacity. We are "unable to understand the world . . . [we] have made. . . . [Whiteness, then,] is a cognitive model that precludes self-transparency and genuine understanding of social realities," as Mills says.[10] Reader, I've been there.

Giving up (or trying to give up) that cognitive model that blinds me to my own conformism is like trying to wake up from a spell. Spelling out the spell *as* white supremacist antichrist poltergeist became essential to me when watching people I admired much of my life react to the affirmation, "Black Lives Matter," as a threat to civilization. A reigning reactivity among so many of my fellow white people drove me to see and recall some of the ways that reactivity once held sway over me and, like the demon spirit is known to do, still shows up, despite frequent personal exorcisms.

As Victor LaValle observes: "Black Lives Matter protests are essentially a national exorcism. If seeing them makes you rage and shake and froth at the mouth, maybe you've got a demon in you."[11] Apocalypse brings long-dormant or effectively self-submerged fears to the surface. Every force evolves a form. Enmity and anger crave a voice. All that hell has to go somewhere.

But there's more than one way to conduct an exorcism upon people and systems, more than one way to overcome fear within ourselves and others, more than one way to wrestle against the infrastructures of bad economics and agreements that we create and that possess and traumatize us. Michael Eric Dyson offers a prognosis and a prescription: "It is my faith that helps me see how whiteness has become a religion. The idolatry of whiteness and the cloak of innocence that shields it can only be quenched by love, but not merely, or even primarily, a private, personal notion of love, but a public expression of love that holds us all accountable. Justice is what love sounds like when it speaks in public."[12]

Circling back to my unflattering memory of my reactive response to the talk back at a screening of *Do the Right Thing* and the path I almost went down, I can recall clearly how a sense of white grievance was beginning to take root and was uprooted, here and there, and planted and uprooted again, here and there, over time by those who held a door open for me, privately and publicly and often lovingly, when I was in danger of mistaking Rush Limbaugh's heat for illumination.

It's a slow and tender process, though, because fear of rejection exercises great power over human hearts. When I look at my students, many of whom have their own Limbaugh equivalents in the form of media personalities like Ben Shapiro, Matt Walsh, Tucker Carlson, and Jordan Peterson, I have to keep in mind that demagogues attract a following for a reason. They offer what feels like strength and belonging among those who've felt outclassed, belittled, and shut down; clobbered by complexity. Toxic personalities are traumatized personalities. And the market for people hoping to triumph over their own trauma shows no signs of disappearing. Hell abhors a vacuum.

But here again, the dark forces I spy *out there* remain *in here* within me. In my teaching as in the rest of life, it's the reality of personal relationships that saves everything, as Merton instructs. Our experiences differ, but I have known their fear of rejection, and I will have to hold mine out with open hands. Tenderness, in this sense, is my superpower. Coupled with caution and curiosity.

Arthur C. Brooks has a word for the challenge and the need for nimbleness: "When we experience exclusion or rejection, the brain's pain centers are activated. In fact, the brain processes relational rejection the same way it processes physical pain."[13]

I don't have to hear that twice. I've felt it. Yes, justice is a form of love. But it might feel like an exorcism at first. The responsive self has to be coaxed out of the armor of reactivity from time to time. Always? Transformative experiences don't often feel easy or painless all the way through. Intersections are hard. They require a maximizing of presence and all available soul. Sometimes we don't need to be pushed. We just need to be sat with.

Is this thing on? Am I prepared to sit (or stand) with myself and others in the reality of personal relationships? Am I present for the exorcisms without and within?

Love as a form of public accountability requires fleshing out. I have a name for such moves already undertaken and underway and yet to be conceived. And yes, it involves exorcism and robots but also radical hospitality. It involves naming the cults within culture. It involves surfacing the responsive self and sometimes loving moves calling out to the responsive self in someone else. For me, robot soft exorcism is a new description for an old and infinite game. You should check this out.

5

Robot Soft Exorcism

The unbearable lightness of playing human

There are so many ways to lose oneself in what can feel like a sea of reactivity. But there are also so many ways to access our center and respond creatively and even beautifully to one another. There are so many ways to be social. Think John Lewis, Tank Man, LeBron James, Fred Rogers, Bree Newsome, and Patti Smith. Think of where other people's kindness has brought you.

The late theoretician of nonviolence Gene Sharp had it right: "No two cases of nonviolent action are alike."[1] The responsive self surfaces, and transformation occurs. Not always but sometimes. And when nonviolent action is met with contempt, there's helpful data here too. I have an example.

In June 2018 there was an incident between then White House press secretary Sarah Huckabee Sanders and Stephanie Wilkinson, the coowner of the Red Hen, a farm-to-table restaurant in Lexington, Virginia. There was a disagreement, and there was also a certain power differential. It caught my attention and got me mulling.

Sanders arrived at the Red Hen with a party of eight in the thick of a troubling news cycle. This was the height of the Trump administration's decision to forcibly separate migrant families as they approached the southern border and a ban on transgender people serving in the military. Staff were stressed at the sight of Sanders and wondering what their responsibilities were in terms of receiving their place of employment as a safe space. Could they refuse service? The Red Hen chef phoned Wilkinson, who then met with her team to figure out together what they were comfortable with. They concluded they could not, in good conscience, continue to serve Sanders, given her public posture and the position she then occupied in a White House they considered corrupt and unsafe.

According to Wilkinson's account, she spoke to Sanders privately, politely requesting that Sanders leave. Sanders said she understood and complied with Wilkinson's wish, and Wilkinson told the party that the appetizers they'd already enjoyed were on the house. Consider the door momentarily held open, the space of mutual genuineness conjured for a spell, a space in which Sanders accepted, at least for a moment, the invitation to be a little less estranged from her center.[2]

The next morning, Sanders took to her government Twitter account:

"Last night I was told by the owner of Red Hen in Lexington, VA to leave because I work for @POTUS and I politely left. Her actions say far more about her than about me. I always do my best to treat people, including those I disagree with, respectfully and will continue to do so."[3]

Protesters, hate mail, and public smearing of the Red Hen by President Trump followed. The restaurant was forced to close for nearly two weeks due to security concerns.[4] This got me thinking about postures, positions, and the wide array of possibilities we each have before us for attempting love in the direction of public accountability. There's data here.

As I see it, Wilkinson did her employees and Sanders a deep kindness. It's worth noting that Sanders herself, though famous, was, at least on paper, a public servant in her capacity as press secretary, a role that involves the oversight of We the People of the United States of America. The Red Hen team was exercising moral due diligence when Sanders crossed their threshold. For her part, Wilkinson tried to play human, speaking as one human being to another, respectfully requesting that Sanders honor a boundary her team asked to be drawn. It might have ended there at the intersection, where self-respecting citizens in the service industry communicated what they required to maintain their own sense of propriety and were met with respect.

The news broke and . . . things took a turn. It seems to me that Sanders mistook her position in the White House for her own person and identity. She used her position and the powers with which she was entrusted to bring Wilkinson and the Red Hen down a notch. Wielding the press secretary Twitter account, Sanders announced that she was herself targeted for working *for* the president (*not*, we might notice, the American people) and thereby took aim at the Red Hen staff's livelihood on our dime and our time. Revenge we will perhaps always have with us this side of the flatline. But taxpayer-funded revenge, in the land of the free, is not fate. I don't like paying for other people's grudges or the targeting of citizens. The whole episode bothered me.

We become what we normalize. And to check the momentum of mechanized corruption, we need more acts of civil courage. The Red Hen need not confront state violence alone. We need more and more people to speak and act with the moral clarity and precision Wilkinson of the Red Hen summoned up. We can invite ourselves and others to play human and rethink our positions and our postures within our positions. We can try for a personal approach, meeting the gaze of the alleged opposition and offering, as well as we can, connection, understanding, and an insistent appeal to shared dignity. Doing so, in Wendell Berry's phrasing, "sets a cleansing fire to prejudices and stereotypes, which grow like weeds among our ideals and principles, so that we may see through them to actual human faces."[5] Humanly facing the human face of the other, whatever the conflict, is essential to the moves I have in mind here.

The more I contemplated this tale of attempted accountability, the more it began to look like an exorcism. The more I imagined the positions in play (small business owner versus White House press secretary), the more these positions took on the form of robots. In time, I saw that Stephanie Wilkinson and her staff were up to something akin to what Tank Man attempted with his fellow human beings in Beijing in 1989. The risk levels differed, but it seems to me that in both instances, people were being invited to be their better selves. Robots be damned.

The Robots Aren't People

Consider this metaphor for perceiving the cults within our culture (institutions large and small), our positions within them, and what *playing human* within and despite them might look like. Remember, it's the reality of personal relationships that saves us.

If my desire to maintain a certain overhead over the years left me at the control panel of a giant robot that—I discovered—was working in tandem with other robots to deport people, traumatize children, crush dissent, and destroy the possibility of human thriving for my fellow creatures here, there, and yon, I'd be grateful for and perhaps even welcome someone—*anyone*—who spied me, a living person, staring down from the window of the robot's eyeball socket, and tried to reach me and offer a strategy for exiting the robot before I died inside it *or* who offered instructions for stopping the robots without hurting the people inside them.

The robots are concentrated forms of human effort, whether reactive, responsive or something in between. They are akin to what the apostle Paul referred to as principalities and powers.[6] We call them brands, platforms, parties, offices, businesses, institutions, governments, organizations, and "follower sets." These ways of naming cultures offer language for referring to systemic evil (naming, envisioning, addressing it) without confusing the people themselves (their faces, for instance) for the evil itself. We desperately need this language. "It's all just people," my partner, Sarah, reminds me when I'm ready to storm the palace, break the window, or hit Send.

I need this help when I'm on the verge of mistaking a person for their position within an institution, flesh and blood for the bloodless robot.

I wrestle not against flesh and blood. But I do get a little punchy with our reigning robots. I owe it to the flesh and blood *within* the robots to get punchy. I owe it to myself. This calls for discernment.

With enough care (breathing and speaking slowly) I can choose contemplation over projection, responsiveness over reactivity. I can gather my wits and remember, *the robots aren't people*, but they do contain them. They are, in fact, powered by them. No people, no robots.

No robots, no people?

Kinda sorta. We need to organize ourselves. We need fire departments, libraries, hospitals, and other neighborhood expressions of care. We can't survive alone. These forms of organization are also robots. Like people, they can operate both beautifully and badly. Decisions create culture, which often assumes the form of robots. Good robots are mechanisms for sharing, mutual thriving, and making sacrifices that *serve* people. Bad robots demand the sacrifice *of* people. They run on reactivity, creating trauma that roots down as toxicity. But lest we fall for a needless dualism in our consideration of the robots we sustain with our energies, remember this: these behaviors exist on a spectrum. Again, an institution is a myth with a budget. Institutions are only as good as the stories they tell, the brand or imprint they make, the cultures they house and sustain. Robots undergo transformation, for better or worse, over time. A robot is a process.

Also this: no robot is worthy of absolute devotion.

The People Aren't Robots

In order for our engagement to bend toward love, we have to remember, while confronting and demanding better behavior of the robots, that we're to avoid wrestling *against* the aforementioned flesh and blood, the human beings looking down at us through the window / eye sockets of the robots. The people aren't robots. They're people *like me*. This is something of a mental fight for some of us. A compassion practice. It's exceedingly important to try to address our fellow human beings as something other than their robots, especially if we expect this kind regard from others outside *our* robots.

There are so many ways to invite people to slow the tape, stop at the intersection, rethink their positions, and don again the mantle of the merely human despite what others do with and within and through available robot sponsors. There are so many ways to respect ourselves and others by demanding the baseline moral seriousness of, well, everyone, but especially abusive people who appear in the public eye. We can politely invite them to step out of their robots.

For a short time the Red Hen incident occupied the news cycle. But it made the case anew for nonviolent moves, here and there, publicized and unpublicized. These moves are at the heart of the whole of human culture. They are myriad. This is how it goes in our one human barnyard with all its busy robots and mixed metaphors.

There are so many old, forgotten, new, and not-yet-dreamed-of means for imaginatively and sometimes lovingly overcoming defensiveness and reactivity, for challenging ourselves and others concerning our almost-always-problematic relationships with our robots (which, again, have no life or power apart from the people inside them).

There's calling up administrators and representatives and specifying what we expect of their activity within their robots. There's accepting responsibility and thinking hard about what we do and say and what we allow people to voice aloud in our presence unchallenged, what we abide when we play along to get along. It doesn't have to be a blowup. We can take it slow and not fight enmity with enmity. Soft exorcisms have happened with sit-ins, op eds, carrying signs reminding those within robots they are accountable and not at all helpless. Talking ourselves and others out of our robots takes time.

Sometimes, admit it, we love our robots who are strong and comfy, and some come not only with a squashing power but with healthcare and retirement benefits. They're hard not to love.

Yet the robot doesn't love you back. We want to be loved for who we are, not for our statuses, standings, or positions. We want to be seen and respected. We want others to offer the assurance that they're interested in us apart from the power we seem to have or wield in our robots. When it comes to robots, respect is a subtle game we can feel ourselves losing. And, like frightened children, we sometimes need to be lulled—and perhaps sometimes stage directed—out of hiding. Yes, Sarah Huckabee Sanders was given the invitation and then, by all appearances, returned to a place of fear and restlessness and hiding behind the eye of the robot after having initially respected her employers' (I mean here her taxpaying, fellow creatures') boundaries.

It didn't have to go that way, and, even now, she need not remain there. Neither need we. We are each accorded the power of circling back, revisiting our blowups, and trying to make things right. To never circle back is to risk losing the capacity for self-reflection. To never circle back is its own little hell. But perhaps the gates of hell are locked from the inside.

Robots get stuffy. They're no place to live out an entire life.

But again, human behaviors within robots (which add up to the behavior *of* robots) exist along a spectrum. Robot soft exorcism theory helps us spy out, analyze, and act imaginatively upon our common compromised reality: the host of hidden structures and tacit social arrangements that draw us away from ourselves and threaten to turn us slowly into what we decry in others. Robot soft exorcism theory, of course, gives witness to the practice, ever ancient and ever new, which is simultaneously a struggle, an ethic, a witness, and a spirit that invites us out the infinite loop of normalizing harm and into effecting true change for ourselves and the worlds we inhabit. Soft exorcism looks like Ella Baker, Diane Nash, Greta Thunberg, and every good teacher we've ever had who held ground and spoke out about power and hiding and how to stop being bound by the robot machine.

It turns out our teachers are everywhere, and the opportunities for robot soft exorcism are all around us. We can be the beloved community (the politics, the media, the broadcast, the witness) we want to see in the world. One specifically non-robot-mediated human interaction at a time, we can present our unarmored selves to one another and inspire gradual or sudden removal of armor. It happens all the time. It's often more than a little bit therapeutic. The healing game is all around us. Think Jesus of Nazareth before Pontius Pilate. Authentic human being is asserting itself in the presence of hardened human being somewhere—many somewheres—even now. Hearts to hearts.

Let's Compare Robots

When we make time to remember and take stock, we each know in our hearts (*places hand on heart*) what's been wrongly normalized in our own presence in the past, what we once sat still and silent for and, depending on our contexts, must prepare to *not* sit still and silent for again. This calls for a contemplative posture in which silence, a little paradoxically, perhaps, can prove generative. Even a few seconds of silence can help avoid our acting on a reactive mind. But it's also the case that a few minutes of silence are just what's needed to realize that it's high time to stand up or speak up.

When I contemplate my context and my resources, I can read the room and understand the human assignment. I can know my own capacities for righteous words and righteous actions. I can see the prophetic tasks in front of me.

At the risk of straining the mechanics of this metaphor past the breaking point, I'd like to take a moment to name a few of my robots, the armored vehicles that aren't me, exactly, but which are each involved in and to some degree occasion this communication. Robot soft exorcism theory helps us see, know, and understand our own situatedness, overcoming the myth of critical detachment. It names a form of good trouble and creative maladjustment, which serves as a calling *in* as opposed to a calling *out.* We are, after all, each of us, situated and embedded *somewhere*.

Here are some of my robots. We might share a few:

- The US government. I don't run the thing, but I'm a citizen and a stakeholder.
- The beautiful state of Tennessee. It's a mess, but it's my mess.
- Downtown Presbyterian Church (PCUSA) in Nashville. Let's call it a community.
- The Dark family. A lively pack of relations I draw upon and in whom I take great pride.
- Belmont University. At this juncture I hold the position of associate professor of religion and the arts.
- Broadleaf Books. (*Waves from within this book.*) The publisher of this book.

- My Substack (Dark Matter). A digital outpost on which I can publish almost anything I want to.
- The tiny robot that is my Twitter account (while it lasts). It is, among other things, a bulletin board, a cry for love, a promotional tool, an influence campaign, and a weapon of mass distraction.

We all have our robots. They're entities, assets, resources, and cultures all at once. How we name and conceive them matters. To take stock of and talk about them is to become more deeply acquainted with our own moral power, what we make of it and how we attend to it.

Once I saw nonviolent action as robot soft exorcism, I found it hard to unsee. I now see it pretty much everywhere.

"[Mitch McConnell,] why do women have to bare their whole soul to you and share their stories & you won't listen?"[7] This tweet summarizes the question Tracy Corder of Oakland, who is currently a campaign director at Action Center on Race and the Economy, asked as McConnell traveled in the wake of the Kavanaugh hearings. He quickened his pace, ignored her, and tried to make his way through an airport and into a black vehicle that would muffle her voice and speed his escape. Disgracing himself and betraying his oath and his baptism, he refused to regard her as a moral equal worthy of his attention. He disgraced himself further by risking appointing an unrepentant sexual predator to the Supreme Court. Why would he risk doing something like this? Robots want what robots want.

"Recounting trauma is powerful but emotionally taxing. It is perhaps more so when the person you are recounting it to won't look you in the eye, refuses to shake your hand or walks into a bathroom to ignore you."[8] That's Maria Gallagher describing her attempt to share her testimony as a sexual assault survivor to a hand-wringing Jeff Flake, who managed a pained look for the camera but joined his Senate colleagues in locking arms around Brett Kavanaugh to protect him against every form of moral accountability. They stuck to the scripts they had to so they could please their robots and maintain their spots within them. While Gallagher's and Corder's appeals to baseline moral seriousness, in one sense, failed, they also offer up data on what crushingly wealthy white men who enable corruption think of as public service. Now we know. Exorcisms have a way of heightening the awareness of all involved parties.

You Never Want to Delegitimize People *Themselves*

Robot soft exorcism may begin with one voice, one person, one stand, but it can prove contagious.

Greta Thunberg, remember, went it alone initially at the age of fifteen, skipping school and sitting outside the Swedish parliament bearing witness against the fecklessness of her elders. "No one was really interested," she explains, "so I had to do it alone. . . . The second day, people started joining me."[9] This is the way it often goes. In time, a British band called the 1975 would invite her to step into their robot and record a vocal for the opening of their album *Notes on a Conditional Form* (2019). They wanted in on her act. Association, we understand, is currency.

Think, too, of activists across the country who've seen fit to surround vans driven by agents of ICE (US Immigration and Customs Enforcement) and obstruct and impede the deportations of our fellow human beings with their bodies. And recall Ian Madrigal, who has dressed up as the Monopoly Man, donning a monocle, to bear witness on C-Span. Ian's appearance on camera puts a visual question mark next to the ritual normalization of billionaires behaving badly in meetings of the House Judiciary Committee. The right costume at the right time can inspire large and small rethinks concerning our preferred robots. Ian notes a threading of the needle at the heart of robot soft exorcism: engage but don't humiliate. Listen: "You never want to delegitimize people themselves, but if you delegitimize their leaders and the ideas that cause suffering in the world, I think people move away from those leaders and ideas."[10]

One can delegitimize a position without demonizing a person, even though the impulse to demonize is strong. It's a form of domination that can feel satisfying in the short term, but, for students of robot soft exorcism, it's a temptation that must be resisted.

Starhawk has an essential word for us here. She notes the difference between "power-over" and "power-with." Power-over is simply more domination. To try to use domination as a tool is to be somehow ineluctably dominated by it. Power-with, however, invites the ostensible opponent's posture and, eventually, their position, to be changed by a creative interaction. The possibility of transformation is at the heart of the beckoning of robot soft exorcism.

Power-over is derived from an ugly conception of other people, which is inextricably bound to an ugly conception of oneself. Power-with disrupts this shame spiral. Consider this:

> Power-over is maintained by the belief that some people are more valuable than others. Its systems reflect distinctions in value. When we refuse to accept those distinctions, refuse to automatically assume our powerlessness, the smooth functioning of the systems of oppression is interrupted. Each interruption creates

a small space, a rip in the fabric of oppression that has the potential to let another power [power-with] come through.

. . . To resist domination, we must act in ways that affirm value—even in our opponents.

We can begin by valuing ourselves, refusing to administer our own oppression.[11]

Robot soft exorcism is like a foot in the door, only requiring the smallest of holds to conjure a way through, banking everything on specific acts of risky self-respect that, every now and then, give rise to shared respect, which, before we know it, conjures a space of mutual respect and, therefore, unforeseen moral realizations. As Marc Halpin observes, "Specificity causes people to pause."[12] To approach a tech billionaire or a country music star or Tucker Carlson in a restaurant or an elected official on their way to their yacht to ask them to slow their roll or to think harder about what their abusive behaviors are doing to non-millionaires is to try to stage a righteous pause. So much begins with a pause, a sense that there might be something lovelier afoot in our experience of others than our fearful, reactive projections allow us to see.

But this requires great subtlety, nuance, nimbleness, and discernment *even if* it involves, as it sometimes must, shouting and scolding. Again, as Starhawk instructs, this is the operation of *power-with* as opposed to *power-over.* It's alarmingly easy to find ourselves administering our own oppression by giving in to enmity and rancor in these moments. The job is to risk, sometimes with fear and trembling, presenting oneself as an unarmored human in the path of well-armored interests (see the robots?) that encase other humans like us. Consider again the eye socket on high and the human being looking down from the control panel. There's a person up there. Perhaps they, too, would welcome some attention, some time in the presence of actual, unafraid faces.

The armored self, after all, always wants to be seen as something more than the armor. We come at each other longing for belonging, desperate with a desire to be known and validated. And our systems, needless to say, are not at all responsive to this longing and desire. We sometimes trick ourselves into imagining they are, as if hoping might make it so. As infinitely valuable bearers of the divine image, we can't seem to help it. As spirit, light, and holiness right out of the womb, hoping is what we do.

Reactivity Can't Drive Out Reactivity

From there, we feel poked, pushed, and bullied and begin to put up defenses, armoring up for all we're worth. That armor builds up and can assume the bulk of a corporation, a celebrity brand, a government, a nation-state, or a best-selling product. Suits of armor come in all sizes. Before we know it, we have ourselves some robots. And yet, part of us desperately wants out. We want to be engaged by real people. We want to be social. We want to be seen and experienced for what we really are.

Which brings us back to reactivity and responsibility. Remember me at intersections? Whether paused at a stop sign, typing words on a screen, or chanting at a protest, my reactive self and my responsive self are present. One of us will surface at any second. I don't always know which one.

I can't speak for anyone but myself, but from what I gather, a responsive self and a creative self are also lurking behind the eyes of my fellow humans at intersections, also sometimes typing words on screens, also situated on one side or the other of an alleged divide. What works for me probably works for them in the strange negotiations that make for life among and within robots. I feel all kinds of emotions during a day, but I can't form helpful thoughts in the direction of meaningful, creative responses until I feel a little relaxed and a little respected.

I say all this to highlight and elaborate upon the "soft" in the exorcism, the drawing out of living human beings, from the figurative but also very real robots that constitute our interlocking cultures. There's certainly a time for calling people *out*. But when we can, we do well to approach conflicts as those who mean to call other people *in* to a better story about themselves and others. Not to power-*over* but to feel empowered. To power-*with* is life itself.

There's an energy that arises within me when I feel looked at curiously and, hopefully, seen. I'm incentivized and enlivened by the expectant gaze. That energy has a way of vanishing when I feel judged or found wanting or, worse, uninvited or in the way or managed. Feelings are subtle that way.

"You're not going to change anybody's mind by shutting them down," Claudia Rankine says.[13] One can't have a realization and feel shut down simultaneously. To try to speak truthfully to a person is to try to speak truthfully to a process. People looking at us out of robots need to be approached with care and caution.

If we don't do this, we'll end up giving energy to something other than the most creative and responsive part of the person we mean to engage. Reactivity can't drive out reactivity. We have to watch what we're emanating. We might not let on, but something within us knows when we're being heard, seen, and respected, when our capacity for truth is being appealed to. When it isn't, there's only fear and more fear, the organized fear that powers the organized violence of our very-much-at-large reigning robots. We strengthen the positions of violent actors when we play into their sense of bodily fear with power-over moves. The key is to hold a door open to power-with. This is how deferential fear is overcome. When I feel invited *onto* a path *out* of fear, all manner of lovely insights become more possible. This is sometimes referred to as an "off-ramp." Sometimes an aggressor is looking for one even as they're behaving aggressively. You can see it in our eyes.

That said, a fellow human at the helm of an abusive robot doesn't have to *feel* attacked to successfully characterize an act of loving candor as an act of aggression. Decreeing an honest plea or a genuine question as an assault on good order is an essential tool in the fascist playbook. One of my most treasured instances of this involved Attorney General Jeff Sessions, who appeared at a Federalist Society luncheon in Boston to speak on the topic of religious liberty in the thick of the Trump administration's family separation policy in 2018.

Exercising his religious liberty, and his due diligence as a Methodist pastor addressing Sessions— also a Methodist—Pastor Will Green of Andover stood up to recite the words of Jesus ("I was hungry and you did not feed me. . . . I was a stranger and you did not welcome me"[14]) and went on to speak the following: "Brother Jeff, as a fellow United Methodist I call upon you to repent, to care for those in need, to remember that when you do not care for others, you are wounding the body of Christ."[15]

Unsurprisingly, Green was forcibly escorted out from the event titled "The Future of Religious Liberty." Sessions followed him with these words: "Well, thank you for those remarks and *attack* . . . I would just tell you we do our best every day to fulfill my responsibility to enforce the laws of the United States."[16] Oh the robots we gather to villainize a courageous pastor. The crowd met Sessions with the desired effect as some booed Green and told him to "Go home!" The tender moment, however, wasn't over.

Dismayed by this response, another person stood up to speak, Darrell Hamilton of Boston. "I thought," he said, "we were here to protect religious liberty."

As Hamilton was then manhandled toward the exit, he narrated what was occurring: "I am a pastor of a Baptist church and you are escorting me out for exercising my religious freedom. That doesn't make sense. It's very hypocritical for this group of people to be going to protect religious freedom while you are escorting me out for doing that very work."[17]

It takes a village to attempt a robot soft exorcism.

You Don't Have to Stay Inside of That Machine

With robot soft exorcism theory, I am very much trying to turn data into metaphor. In this, I am not going it alone. Dustin Kensrue of the band Thrice, together with his bandmates (Teppei Teranishi and Riley and Eddie Breckenridge), has turned this weird little theory into song. Here comes "Robot Soft Exorcism":

> *Looking down through armored glass*
> *Above a field of fire and ash*
> *And from this height it's hard to even tell*
> *Just what it's like outside the suit*
> *The terror, and the torn-up roots*
> *The lives you've helped to make a living hell*
> *But there's another way*
> *To face the unforeseen*
> *You don't have to stay*
> *Inside of that machine*

That's the first verse and the initial chorus, helped by the move of the robot to a kind of paranoid android suit. There's unnatural disaster and fear of the unknown, but there are also, we're assured, alternatives. We are being invited to step out of our vehicles.

> *Staring up across the wreck*
> *A single figure stands erect*
> *They shout and wave, so tiny and absurd*
> *And moved by curiosity*
> *You crack and lift the canopy*
> *And straining you can just make out their words*

There's another way
To face the unforeseen
You don't have to stay
Inside of that machine
There's a bigger game
And there's a deeper dream
You don't have to stay
Inside of that machine

Robot soft exorcism theory is a way of naming and analyzing an everyday practice. It comes down to trying to pique someone else's curiosity, to inspire, if we can, a sense of wonder and even a sense of play. Is there a bigger game afoot? Finite play giving way to infinite play? Having to face the unknown is our universal psychic pickle. But there's a *deeper* dream than the shallow schemes and short-term arrangements we've settled for and succumbed to in these stuffy, nightmare robot suits. And we all need an intervention.

So please, come down now
Come out from where you've been
Please, come down now
Come out and start again

I know you're scared
But so are we

And if you dare
You'll start to see
There's another way
To face the unforeseen
You don't have to stay
Inside of that machine

It's a tender (soft), intentional, and interior work. It's a group activity because with common dreams come feats of group discernment and acts of group courage. This is how we overcome systemic evils together. One inviting gesture at a time. One person exiting the robot at a time.

"A dream often undermines the narratives of power and winning," Fanny Howe writes.[18] We desperately need such dreams. They restore the senses. Dreams show us what we're hiding from ourselves. They help us think through our projections, our reactions, and our responses. Dreams help us consider the question of how to know what we want, what we really—I mean really—want.

There Is No *Them*

I am not the first to dream of robots. It's a common trope. Ironically enough, Sarah Huckabee Sanders (now governing—in a manner of speaking—the state of Arkansas) once deployed it in a heated exchange with George Stephanopoulos over her decision to publicly push the suggestion that "countless" FBI agents had joined her (and Donald Trump) in the insistence that there was "no collusion" with the Russian government on the part of the Trump campaign in the 2016 presidential election. Stephanopoulos invited her to reflect aloud on her own habitual devotion, in these moments, to "a culture of lying." It's not "a slip of the tongue," he observed but rather "a deliberate false statement."

Attempting a deflection, also a form of live-action dissociation, Sanders insisted, "It was in the heat of the moment. Meaning that it wasn't a scripted talking point." She added with the sneer: "I'm sorry that I wasn't a robot like the Democrat Party."[19]

It's not *you*, it's *them* is true if by "them," we're referring to our robots. There is no *them*, as the healing mantra has it. There's only you and me. There's only the flesh and blood, the beating hearts, of you and me and all of us. The all-too-human beings.

We are, let's admit it, in this robot situation together. I, too, get all up in my binaries. I overreact and make poor choices that (as choices will) create and sustain toxic cultures. When I'm feeling defensive, I even embrace the occasional falsehood that—if I give it voice—will take the form of false statements, which means I'm conjuring and sustaining a culture of lying. It isn't me, it's . . . the paranoid android within?

"I wasn't a robot" or "I'm not a robot" can be healing mantras, too, insofar as they're positive affirmations of my own humanity. "That wasn't me" can be a helpful confession insofar as it's a starting point for further unpacking: "That's not who I want to be." "My best self didn't show up just then. I'd like to try again, okay?" "Something that isn't me got a hold of me."

We confuse ourselves for our robots every so often. For my own part, I've even changed my shape and size to fit the demands of particular robots. I didn't realize that was what was happening at the time. I sometimes confuse fitting in for belonging. Robots offer security, but often at the cost of a considerable degree of soul.

The fact is this: "Conscience, like creation, cannot be hurried. It cannot even be scheduled."[20] That's James Blish in a work of science fiction. Among our best novelists, he knows something about people and their tools.

"Robot soft exorcism" manages, it seems to me, to serve the work of naming what we're going through or hiding within. Like White Supremacist Antichrist Poltergeist, it helps me acknowledge more reality than I'm generally comfortable with, but I owe it to myself and others to accept and act on more reality as I age. It's my job as a fellow creature citizen to try to become more real. I see robot soft exorcism everywhere. Which is to say I see avenues for authentically human behavior almost everywhere. Don't you?

The challenge, then, is to err on the side of behaving like a human being. Maybe there is no error in behaving like a human being ever. Maybe what we lose by behaving humanly is something we'd have to lay down eventually anyway. There comes a time to step away from our vehicles.

"But we must never forget that there is something within human nature that can respond to goodness, that [humankind] is not totally depraved; to put it in theological terms, the image of God is never totally gone."[21] This is Dr. King offering us a way of thinking through the divine image in everyone. I try to hold to it.

Even in the face of alarming violations of moral norms, there is something within the aggressor that *can respond to goodness*. We can appeal to it. We have to. If we don't respond to the moral betrayals occurring around us, our consent is complicit. We owe it to each other to step in, stand up, and speak up when someone within our ambit is morally debasing themselves. We can search out the human face within the robot. In the reality of personal relationships, transformation remains possible.

Just because someone acts like a cartoon character doesn't mean we have to treat them like one. In fact, to the extent that I myself behave like an unhinged cartoon character, it's my prayer that people will address me with love and firmness. To address me as someone harming others or myself. That is, from what I can tell, a space in which the soul resides. That space is our human inheritance. We risk losing it if we become what we normalize.

As Daniel Berrigan says:

> Living humanly has a price attached. Let us pay up, and gladly. Knowing as well that the opposite, living inhumanly, pays huge dividends in a crooked world.
>
> Celebrate then, the burden.[22]

For real. Celebrate it. Step out of the machines. See the deeper dream. Dream it.

6

Beyondism

Dwelling above the fray of observational candor

According to family lore, my dad once walked into a Sunday School class where most everyone was complaining about the fact that a popular and allegedly obscene film was currently being screened in Nashville.

"Have any of you seen it?" he asked. They admitted that none of them had.

"Well, I have," he said, "and y'all don't know what you're talking about."

My dad knew how to touch a nerve, something I loved and admired him for. This nerve-touching seems to have formed my personality more than a little and has lately surfaced again as I've entered into some lively exchanges with friends and strangers.

Like many Americans, in recent years I've found myself feeling more than a little estranged from friends and acquaintances I've known and trusted for much of my life. I've also found myself being regarded suspiciously by a handful of fellow adults who, in other seasons, have happily vouched for me as a solid and trustworthy person.

At fifty-three, I'm being invited to enter more fully into a deeper awareness of the life I share with the world. The rifts can mean I'm not as useful or even dependable to some as I once was. Perhaps I can't be counted on to say the predictable things I once said. My story is changing. I am reckoning with whiteness in a new way. I'm deferring to my now-grown children on all kinds of matters. I'm thinking harder about injustice.

"Injustice should never bore you," Claudia Rankine once asserted.[1] Trying to discern, address, and overcome injustice is essential, as I see it, to my own mental health. Ignoring it is boring as hell.

No one is not political. Yet the leveling of the word *political* at a person or a situation is, it seems, a handy trick for drawing our attention away from incoming data and unflattering facts. The optics, after all, are the optics.

With words we use to accuse, like *politics*, we can steer clear of every form of moral accountability. We can pretend and persuade others that politics is a thing that only involves other people. Unpleasant folks who are *partisan*, as the saying goes, and therefore "polarizing." "Politics" as a thing *I'm* not playing is a rhetorical weapon that's proven especially useful to career politicians, their preferred pundits, and the anonymous donors who control them. Is tragipoetic a word? It should be.

The word I use for the posture whereby one speaks of oneself as operating outside of politics and thereby capable of opining and weighing in magically above the fray: *beyondism*. Beware the beyondist persona.

We have discussed the beautiful possibilities available to each of us in the form of "robot soft exorcism," which again is only funny-sounding shorthand for this: avenues for authentically human behavior.

Our task—as well as invitation—is this: behave like human beings among human beings.

Beyondism, when meeting with that task, responds, "Now is not the time for politics." Have you heard that one? Have you, perchance, offered that diversion technique?

It comes to us from every arena, including utterances from elected officials—some of them millionaires—whose every material need is met by the American taxpayer, especially when those officials are publicly blocking citizens' access to our own money and resources. (*Waves from Tennessee)*

The idea that "politics" is a thing any human being ever steps in and out of is beyondism. It is also a tool of white supremacist terror. You can respectfully address a man in a tie and still insist that he behave like an adult. Such insistence doesn't mean someone suddenly *got political*, and it need not be construed as an attack, a blast, a slam, or an attempt to cancel anyone. Insisting on better behavior of people with whom we're in momentary or constant relationship is part of emotional literacy, the everyday, relatively common effort, we might say, of observational candor. And as I see it, observational candor is often a form of love.

But beyondism resists. It's a way of immunizing ourselves against this love with a peculiar posture that can easily be mistaken for self-respect. It can be beheld on social media when someone inscribes their alleged conviction that some things can't be meaningfully discussed on social media. This out-of-body rhetorical tool is the beyondist persona, that strange disavowal of my own presence *within* the social world, which is also, paradoxically, an assertion that my own presence is *more substantial* than—or functions differently from—the presence of others.

Always political, but not just for the realm of politicians, beyondism is also a form of forgetfulness in which a journalist, an administrator, a pundit, a preacher, or an elected official loses sight of the fact that they're somebody in a body like everyone else and that their real peers are their fellow human beings.

Authentic Humanness Is Good Politics

"Who do you credit and why?" is a question the journalist Jessica Hopper taught me to put to myself and others.[2] The more I repeat it aloud, the more beyondist thinking loses its hold, the more I feel my own presence as someone whose speech, inquiry, and action can make a real difference for people with whom I share a world. It's a very good feeling. "Who do you credit and why?" is the kind of question that serves to overcome deferential fear. It also leads to a very good feeling.

Beyondism doesn't credit and won't enter the realm of the human. In the final analysis, it's not a very good feeling. It banks everything on estrangement fused with domination—a moral dead end because it's based on the myth of critical detachment.

Charging others with being hysterical or hyper-partisan or filled with rage while insinuating that a frenzy is afoot on "both sides," the beyondist will never own their own thinking or doing. In some contexts the beyondist persona might seem even mostly harmless, but it shows up as no help at all during a pandemic or when a white supremacist terror regime is trying to overturn the results of an election. "Partisanship" can only go so far when it comes to naming the threats to public safety posed by a poltergeist and its host bodies.

When we block out of our own lives the lives of those our own words and actions have messed with, we take privilege, a luxury unavailable to most people, to beyondism. We mistake it for strength and influence even as we use its operations: gatekeeping, gaslighting, and feigning neutrality. Beyondism uses forms of abuse and estrangement with a scrim of professionalism, leadership, and gravitas in its strict adherence to the myth of critical detachment, which is perhaps the most dangerous myth of all.

As I understand the human situation, no person is more or less political than anyone else. We're all here, trying to get a life in one way or another, and hopefully paying attention to what our words and actions bring about. Authentic humanness is good politics. Beyondism, declining to view yourself as a human being among other human beings and behaving accordingly, is bad politics. Beyondism trivializes our common humanity and the righteous possibilities before us. And our call as humans for humanizing ourselves involves resisting, without and within, all its forms.

Grace Paley has a word: "The slightest story ought to contain the facts of money and blood in order to be interesting to adults. That is, everybody continues on this earth by courtesy of certain economic arrangements. . . . Trivial work ignores these two facts and is never comic or tragic."[3]

Fear No Theory

Maybe you, like me, want to get our story straight. To see clearly, stay healthy, not hurt anyone, and remain interesting to others. In recent years, I've noted three words that, when placed together, alarm many of my heretofore generally unperturbed peers with an intensity I didn't see coming: *critical race theory*.

Like my father before me, I think it's important to know something about what you're talking about before you condemn, malign, or outlaw it.

Words with which to wave away an incoming moral realization we have always had with us—critical race theory is all of that and more and somehow different. Governor Bill Lee, the father of three of my former students, recently banned it (without defining it) in my state's public schools. Mike Pence recently took a public swipe at it (without defining it). The government of Texas has also banned it (without defining it).

"The name Critical Race Theory, now used as interchangeably for race scholarship as Kleenex is for tissue, was basically made up, fused together to mark a possibility," Professor Kimberlé Williams Crenshaw offers in a beautiful lowdown. She adds, "The notion of CRT as a fully unified school of thought remains a fantasy of our critics."[4] Have you noticed?

Beyondists, we've come to understand, are easily triggered. And White Supremacist Antichrist Poltergeist is easily spooked.

Here's my take: theory is just thinking. Critical thinking is just thinking carefully (not negatively). Critical race theory is thinking carefully and out loud about race. Critical race theory is gospel (good news). Let's receive it. Let's have the conversations out loud. Fear no theory!

Critical race theory names a body of work—it's important to keep that in mind as our legislatures (and some universities) try to ban it. Did you ever think this day would come? The banning of thought? Of conversation? If you've made it this far and you're upset with me and you're about to tell someone that I embrace critical race theory, please listen closely.

I can't—no one can—embrace critical race theory any more than we can embrace a library. We'd have to read it all first. I can't even critique a theory exactly. I can only address a person voicing it, one sentence at a time. Like we do with Bible verses and films and poetry and legal documents, we need to read words, mull them, ask one another what we think those words mean, feel something, *change our minds*, double back, feel differently, and then think it through again. Before anyone can begin to know where anyone stands on something as broad and voluminous as critical race theory, we need to open books and cite texts and live the conversations and the questions. From there one can get a sense of what a person, a volume of that library, an author is saying. You can't step in the same sense twice.

Even then when we read, say, one person's book or article, we're only talking about one critical race theorist's course of thought, which, as these things go, will differ from the courses of thought of other critical race theorists. We're dipping into a vast collection of witnesses. Do they all say the same thing? Of course not. Interested parties can read them to develop an examined opinion on the subject.

Somebody quoting Dr. Ibram X. Kendi doesn't mean they (or anyone) has gotten to the bottom of critical race theory. It just means they've quoted Ibram X. Kendi. Was he quoted in a way that honors the full context of what he is (or was) on about? You'd have to look up the quote and read him to find out. My fifties have been a surprising education, an apocalypse, really, in who is and isn't willing to do that. Yet myriad white people my age—who seem to understand that we become what we normalize— are starting anti-racist book clubs. By the way, anti-racist book clubs, especially when they're conducted around a fire during a global pandemic, are a clear and present danger to the beyondist persona.

Many have started with Kendi for good reason. In an alarmingly inviting way, he speaks of anti-racism as a journey he's still on and one along which he's desirous of company. I've developed a habit of sharing some of Kendi's words with anyone I imagine might be open to receiving them. To my delight, getting people to hear his words has defused a situation or two (as reading thoughtful prose aloud often can). If you're reading this and someone's threatened to cut you out of their will or have you fired or denied funding because they think you think you're a "woke" proponent of critical race theory, ask them to consider these words, maybe pray about their decision, and then take it from there. Among his words are those on the subject of being "fooled by racist ideas" and then where he once was in his process:

> I did not fully realize that the only thing wrong with Black people is that we think something is wrong with Black people. I did not fully realize that the only thing extraordinary about White people is that they think something is extraordinary about White people. . . .
>
> When you truly believe that the racial groups are equal, then you also believe that

the racial disparities must be the result of racial discrimination. Committed to this antiracist idea of group equality, I was able to self-critique, discover, and shed the racist ideas I had consumed over my lifetime while I uncovered and exposed the racist ideas that others have produced over the lifetime of America. I know that readers truly committed to racial equality will join me on this journey of interrogating and shedding our racist ideas.[5]

At the very least, we can start with our own humanity and some words. At the very least you won't find yourself defending a critically unexamined abstraction (CRT) that, I sometimes suspect, is mostly a placeholder for a raw sense of powerlessness at the thought that someone(s) somewhere thinks you're racist.

Fellow white people, a word to you directly. Beyondism isn't limited to whiteness, but whiteness is definitely where beyondism shows up, in my experience, most often. Let's humanize ourselves, step out of our robots, and acknowledge that when we let our fellow white people speak derisively of other people's thoughtfulness in our presence without challenging them, we're complicit in the terror that follows. That thing where you think you'd have behaved differently in Nazi Germany or Apartheid South Africa or the Jim Crow era? Then is now. The government of Georgia has criminalized giving bottled water to dehydrated voters. Then is now.

Beauty Prepares the Heart for Justice

The avenues for authentic humanness are everywhere. Consider the American contralto Marian Anderson standing and singing beautifully in front of the Lincoln Memorial in April 1939.

Hear this: the Daughters of the American Revolution did not have the words "critical race theory" available as a rhetorical weapon with which to shut down the testimonies of people of color, but they did have the power to deny her the opportunity to sing in the DAR Constitution Hall. When they did, Eleanor Roosevelt gave up her spot among them, and Anderson was soon invited to perform a concert on the steps of the Lincoln Memorial for an integrated audience.[6] The humanity in attendance stretched out as far as the eye could see. Record crowds.

Beauty prepares the heart for justice. And popular culture eats white supremacist terror for breakfast. Think of Mike and Karen Pence enjoying a performance of *Hamilton*, being publicly admonished by the cast,[7] taking it, and still maybe imagining that they might yet partner with civil society in November

2016. That was a robot soft exorcism. If I could access them, I'd ask if they felt a little less like beyondists that night. I wonder if they feel like beyondists now.

It's never too late to turn away from evil. I want to try to persuade myself, my students, and all of us to lean toward the witness of Marian Anderson, who braved threats to her life to lift her voice, and Eleanor Roosevelt, who made a break with white supremacist terror at a decisive moment. Is recalling these events critical race theory?

Another act of risky humanness is Bree New-some's prophetic act of conscience following the Mother Emanuel terror attack in Charleston. It was June 2015. She was very specific as she ascended the pole outside the South Carolina State House to remove the Confederate flag: "In the name of Jesus, this flag has to come down. You come against me with hatred and oppression and violence. I come against you in the name of God. This flag comes down today."[8] She was assisted by a man at the base of the pole named James Ian Tyson who overheard a policeman muse aloud that he might tase her. Seeing the lethal threat, Mr. Tyson hugged the pole and told the officer that doing so would likely electrocute both of them. The policeman backed off. Both Newsome and Tyson were arrested. Ms. Newsome recited a psalm. The white supremacist terror idol was up again in forty-five minutes.[9]

If those in the corridors of power who wish to ban critical race theory prevail, the suppression of these facts of history will come next.

Ms. Newsome comes to mind as I contemplate the alive and signaling prophetic witness. As we think through what beyondism, the coddling of white supremacist operatives, has cost us.

We Become What We Let Slide

The 2017 Episcopal Statement from the Council of Bishops of the African Methodist Episcopal Church rings a clear bell on the cost:

> We ask that every member of this denomination, and people who are committed to justice and righteousness, equality and truth, will join with us to thwart what are clearly demonic acts. Indeed, the words of the Apostle Paul to the believers at Ephesus apply today, "for we wrestle not against flesh and blood, but against [. . .] the rulers of the darkness of this [world], against spiritual wickedness in high places."
>
> President Trump has demonstrated that his word is not to be trusted or believed.[10]

The statement has been sitting on the internet for years. The prophetic leadership addressing spiritual wickedness afoot in America is all around us, along-side the prevailing evasiveness of the beyondist gatekeepers. Is the specificity of it too partisan? Too polarizing? Would publicizing and discussing it diminish clicks, followers, sales, support, ad revenue? Are white God talkers in America afraid that publicly deferring to the AME Church would diminish their brands?

We have a longer history of the present with which to contend. It's time to consider and receive the witness of the prophets already among us.

Witness Tami Sawyer of Memphis (Shelby County Commissioner) addressing the public concerning the relocation of a monument and the remains of Mary Ann Montgomery and Nathan Bedford Forrest in June 2021. It was the hard-won culmination of Saw-yer's long campaign to reclaim a public park for the people of Memphis. Behind her threatened George "K-Rack" Johnson, a volunteer from the Sons of Con-federate Veterans, singing "Dixie." Addressing the crowd, Sawyer said, "We are not post-racial America. We are not post-racial Memphis. This hatred and this racism is large and loud." Then, addressing Johnson, she added, "I bet you do wish you were 'in the land of cotton.'"[11]

We become what we normalize. We become what we let slide.

At least a few of the politicians, pundits, and pas-tors in Tennessee normalized the alleged threat of critical race theory, normalized George Johnson and those who publicly derided Tami Sawyer and threatened her life. This is what normalizing does: news of George Johnson's tirade led to a cascade of new threats from people publicly emboldened to target Sawyer further. Tennessee's Republican supermajority remained silent on the matter. The beyondist normalizing impulse is strong. It's in our elected officials, their church organizations, and us who stand silent, in our sheep herds, in all who will not cross "K-Rack" or risk his ire.

For her part, Sawyer posted these private threats online. Doing so is an act of public service: "We are wasting our time arguing about bonnets and white women are calling our locs snakes. I'm going to keep sharing these because our natural state of inertia needs to be disrupted. (Inertia: a tendency to do nothing or to remain unchanged.)"[12] We can't address what we won't see.

The beyondists and normalizers among us (and we ourselves) are hanging back as whiteness rampages. For fear, it seems, of losing the well-paid positions from which they can decry "both sides," beyondists have given the critical race theory panic a pass. I now behold people I've loved and respected for much of my life brandishing and enunciating the words "critical race theory" and "woke" in the hope that they've finally named the evil that wants to make people who look like them and me and our children feel bad. It's handy for the normalizers, for the conflict avoidant: just be quiet and let it go.

Normalizers, read Christina Edmondson's essential word: "The middle ground is not holy ground."[13]

Klanmind

Like the brutal fantasy of whiteness, beyondism pays well and dies hard. It builds our sense of reassurance and groupness, our belonging. In this sense, the allure of beyondism, for its practitioners as well as its target markets, is powered by nostalgia. Svetlana Boym is my preferred guide in these waters:

> Nostalgia (from *nostos*—return home, and *algia*—longing) is a longing for a home that no longer exists or has never existed. Nostalgia is a sentiment of loss and displacement, but it is also a romance with one's own fantasy. Nostalgic love can only survive in a long-distance relationship. . . .
>
> . . . The danger of nostalgia is that it tends to confuse the actual home and the imaginary one. In extreme cases it can create a phantom homeland, for the sake of which one is ready to die or kill. Unreflected nostalgia breeds monsters.[14]

I've held this passage close as I've watched Governor Bill Lee push disinformation to drive legislation designed to ban thought, conversation, and reading material that challenge white supremacist terror ideology in public schools. The poet Ed Sanders refers to that ideology as klanmind,[15] a peculiar meanness specific to the southern culture Bill Lee and I share, a perverse conception of self and others that festers under cover of darkness and dollars. Often based in unreflective nostalgia and militant ignorance, klanmind might be a helpful shorthand for Bill Lee's uncritical race theory.

Klanmind is also a helpful word for Christian nationalism, a form of white nationalism, and it's fewer syllables than *White Supremacist Antichrist Poltergeist*. Klanmind promises a phantom homeland, a living death, an unreflective nostalgia.

Reflective nostalgia, on the other hand, can compel us to imagine ourselves and others more artfully. Against beyondism, it can also help us develop and deepen a sense of righteous expectation, a commitment to the deeper dream occasioned and signaled by robot soft exorcism, one ritual among many in the overcoming of deferential fear.

Reflective nostalgia doesn't fear or flee incoming data. With reflection, we can recall, remember, review, and debrief what we've gone through honestly, and, when necessary, repentantly. Everyone's invited to this artfulness.

Reflective nostalgia breeds prophets and critical race theorists. Reflective nostalgia fears no theory.

Prophets are dwellers on thresholds. Healing and dealing. Holding the tension between these opposites: America is a crime scene, a promise, and a living possibility. It is also a long conversation, an extended argument about what human beings owe one another. If we love (or want to love) America, we have to look hard and humbly at the data of where we are lest the argument prove to have been more like a long, catastrophic con.

Our history, as James Baldwin teaches us, can't be bracketed away any more than breathing can be put to the side of speech. We live in and by the fact of what happened: "History is not the past. It is the present. We carry our history with us. We are our history. If we pretend otherwise, we literally are criminals."[16] The work of remembering is the work of awakening to our own lives, our own context. To meaningfully *respond* to available data is to enter a state of *respons*ibility, the lovely and constant task of a responsible people.

To know the felt joy of responsibility is to refuse at every turn the "protective sentimentality,"[17] Baldwin's phrase, that prefers a mythic American innocence over a clear-eyed index of violence perpetuated, suffered, and, from time to time, unmasked in our land's history. To challenge the script of protective sentimentality in an age of white supremacist memory laws can pose certain risks, but these are the very risks that make democracy possible within and in spite of moneyed interests, foreign and domestic, that appear hell-bent on reducing us to a population of passive spectators each alone in our informational echo chambers.

Like reflective nostalgia, critical race theory invites us to wake up to our own context and explore with compassion and curiosity the context of others; the history that is our collective present, the joy that is the reality of other people and of thinking together.

7

Free Reality

Contemplating and pursuing transformative justice

There are stories some people—sometimes we ourselves—don't want told. There's data we rush to hush, belittle, sideline, and diminish. Politics, family gatherings, social media: observe it in in the dismissive shrug, the swift change of topic, and the look that tells me I've brought up a news item I shouldn't have or spoken favorably of a famous person who is, for some reason, on the outs with some or many in the group I'm in. Sometimes I'm in the robot. And sometimes I've been in the robot enough that I can see the robots in their eyes. The shrug tells me everything: no one here will risk their positions, their associations, and the tacit approval of their people group. No one will risk upsetting or losing their spot.

Here in Nashville, that spot can involve a mortgage, access to healthcare, a book deal, a reference letter, or a position in an organization. If you're a high roller, it can involve a board of trustees, a pulpit, a political appointment, a celebrity, or a CEO. This, of course, goes beyond Nashville. The chumocracy is everywhere, that sometimes loose but also sometimes very tight network of millionaires and billionaires and powermongers who, it sometimes seems, avoid conflict with one another for a living. We all have our robots.

> Fellow humanizers, notice what doesn't get said, who gets overlooked, and how particular events don't surface as newsworthy.

Fellow humanizers, notice what doesn't get said, who gets overlooked, and how particular events don't surface as newsworthy. For the media, "newsworthy," in this calculus, refers to what's commercially viable. "Commercially viable" is just whatever will get sufficient ratings (clicks and views) and thereby generate the most ad revenue. Spot the robots in this mix? I do. In this case, it's helpful for me to feel less animosity toward the high rollers who appear on the screen delivering what's referred to as "the news." It *isn't* personal. They're just trying to hold on to their spots. It's a robot system. It's a military-industrial-entertainment-incarceration complex. It is, of course, also a culture.

Decisions—evasions, avoidances, and alliances too—have given us this culture. We become what we normalize.

But this culture isn't fate. It isn't inevitable. Different decisions create different cultures. Cultures within cultures. Robots within robots. Within these arrangements, the job, as I understand it, is to orient ourselves in as alert and artful a fashion as we can and to try to overcome, together with others, every form of deferential fear, opting for awareness at every turn. If our awareness is shaped by the high-tech horse race for ad revenue, assuming responsibility for what we do, say, and share will involve creatively contemplating together with others what it means to know (or claim to know) something. This will call for courage, conscience, and curiosity. This is the prophetic task of a genuinely examined life in an age of disinformation.

Seeking the Healing of All Parties

The more beautiful, just, and integrated path of an examined life might involve returning to a question we considered earlier: Am I responsible for the lies I let others voice in my presence unchallenged? Mulling that one well means thinking hard about context, looking around the room, reading the room, and hearing from people whose experience differs from our own. This, too, is holiness: learning to read and listen to ourselves and others with care and curiosity. These are the brave spaces in which deferential fear can be overcome. Brave spaces appear when and wherever we make time to find ourselves and others interesting and, at the risk of sounding dramatic, beautiful. Beauty prepares the heart for justice.

By justice I don't just mean any old conception of justice. I mean real justice, which, to my mind, is *always* transformative. Transformative justice is the alternative to retaliatory justice (most famously summed up in the phrase "an eye for an eye"). Retaliatory justice is based on the myth of restorative violence, the mad vision according to which violence, applied strategically, can heal and killing can bring wholeness, as if hurt and humiliation serve health and torture and trauma bring peace. Jesus of Nazareth rejected the myth of restorative violence, which is grounded in fear, delusion, and anxiety, and offered with his words, his righteous witness, and his very life the imaginative, prophetic, artful alternative of transformative justice. Unlike retaliatory justice, transformative justice seeks the healing of all parties.

All justice is relational. Transformative justice responds to conflict with candor and conscience, courage and curiosity. Injustice, remember, is no accident. See the setup. Know that it's orchestrated. Say what you're seeing.

And remember to consider the robots. Consider our military-industrial-entertainment-incarceration complex. It's a setup. Whether we're talking about ad revenue, the arms industry, or fossil fuels, the thing runs on deferential fear. We live in its shadow. Except when our hearts prepare us for transformational justice.

Within and among the robots are stories of people who've overcome deferential fear and thereby offered alternatives to these reigning normalizations. I try to collect and amplify and hold them before myself and others as examples, as artisans of moral seriousness. Thinking about them gives me hope and courage and energy. Some I've named and described already, but I've noticed and come to know more over the last few years that I'd like to look at with you.

They have each been targeted and suffered harm by bad-faith actors who largely exist in the shadows, unnamed and unaccountable. I've noticed they've been specifically and consciously passed over—made largely invisible—by the culture I'm calling the military-industrial-entertainment-incarceration complex. Their stories give us an understanding of the tension between what is and what's supposed to be. Telling their stories also helps break the silence demanded of us by roboworld and sets down, in one small way, a new norm.

The tension between what is and what's supposed to be marks any genuine consideration of the witness of Anthony Ray Hinton of Alabama. Wrongfully imprisoned, awaiting execution, and eventually exonerated and set free through the unanimous decision of the Supreme Court after nearly thirty years on death row,[1] Hinton exists among us as a courageous and movingly candid survivor of our state violence, an alive and signaling example of what's wrong with our so-called criminal justice system. His jarringly thorough memoir, *The Sun Does Shine: How I Found Life and Freedom on Death Row*, dropped in 2018 and is an essential resource for anyone at all invested in the dismantling of taxpayer-funded, white supremacist terror and the pursuit of transformative justice in the here and now.

From the moment in 1985 when Hinton, at age twenty-nine, was arrested at his home while mowing his mother's lawn and charged with two counts of capital murder, we encounter an assortment of villains, but, as a narrator studying and reflecting upon his own experience, Hinton never villainizes the people wronging him. Instead he confronts them with a commanding and often charismatic curiosity, chronicling aloud, in court, for instance, their crushingly bad decisions ("You people don't want the truth. . . . All you wanted was a conviction"[2]) as well as his own resolute refusal to fritter away his soul by dwelling in enmity ("I thank God that it came to me that I can't make it into heaven hating nobody"[3]).

By choosing to publicly narrate the torture and trauma carried out upon him, dramatizing the otherwise hidden hypocrisies of judges, lawyers, and law enforcement, Hinton moves between the bardic and the prophetic in his account. In his open-handed, good-humored, and persistent intellectual hospitality under duress, he stands with Fannie Lou Hamer, Nelson Mandela, Mahatma Gandhi, and Socrates, creating a space of inquiry for interlocutors and aggressors alike. At the heart of his method is a conviction he picked up from his mother that, with enough compassion, empathy, and imagination, some form of family can be made to exist anywhere.

This is particularly evident when Hinton describes how he wrested from the warden the right to conduct a book club on death row. Like the guards with whom Hinton developed something akin to friendship, the warden was puzzled and charmed by his forthright friendliness coupled with a resolute unwillingness to suffer foolishness. (For instance, Hinton declined to appear or be addressed on camera when celebrity journalist Geraldo Rivera filmed himself spending the night in a cell.) For the book club, he arranged to accept by mail and distribute copies of Maya Angelou's *I Know Why the Caged Bird Sings* and James Baldwin's *Go Tell It on the Mountain* to be shared, read, and discussed among inmates.[4]

I'd Rather Die for the Truth Than Live a Lie

From there, Hinton conducted civil and even revelatory conversations with men like Henry Hays, convicted and sentenced to death for his role in the lynching of Michael Donald. As they read Baldwin aloud to each other, Hinton says he highlighted this sentence: "For the rebirth of the soul was perpetual; only rebirth every hour could stay the hand of Satan."[5] Following his death by electrocution, Hays, like other departed book club members, was remembered through the setting of an empty chair in the book club.[6]

That gesture reflects a commitment Hinton promised his peers for himself and others: they and he will extend beyond their years of incarceration. "I'm going to tell the world about how there was men in here that mattered. That cared about each other and the world. That were learning how to look at things differently."[7] Hinton held to that promise by refusing the opportunity to accept a life sentence—on the condition he plead guilty to murders he had nothing to do with—when a lawyer working with the Equal Justice Initiative placed it before him. Even if it meant execution is in his future, Hinton was resolved: "I'd rather die for the truth than live a lie."[8] By firing that particular lawyer, he entered into a working relationship with Bryan Stevenson.

The delays of justice were maddening. Even with his innocence essentially proven, the determined denials of well-heeled career public officials in Alabama who wanted to save face above all else kept him caged. Hinton's witness is an ethnographic field study of taxpayer-funded white supremacist terror in Alabama. He's an activist, a scholarly authority on the multi-pronged strategies and interlocking tactics involving courtrooms, journalists, and network news producers that anyone (lawyers, activists, allies) has to undertake to move the needle toward justice when there are no lanes. In the telling of his tale and his determination to find common cause with unlikely others, Hinton endures by being nimble and refusing to reduce his soul to the size of someone else's fear.

Hinton speaks with authority because he speaks from experience, as one horribly wronged by a cascade of lies, of knowingly false witnesses, of unexamined opinions backed by bars and armed force. He is a profoundly inspiring model of what a genuinely examined life looks like and an artisan of moral seriousness.

Hinton is also among our greatest living philosophers, which my friend J. C. Rhee defines as "someone who would rather be homeless and truthful than rich and a liar."[9] Put that way, I am struck by the feeling that I am not much of a philosopher. I know in my bones that, under extremity, I likely *would* lie for a warm bed on a cold night.

But under extremity, Anthony Ray Hinton refused to lie ("I'd rather die for the truth than live a lie."). He would not suppress his own conscience to save his life, what Václav Havel calls "to live within the truth" amid systematized lies.[10] This is the work.

Decisions create culture.

Embodied Solidarity

The stories particular people don't want told always tell a story. Take this story of repressed memories among many talkative white people (and other beyondists) in America. Let this serve as a bit of a trigger warning.

"I've always thought that if more good people had concealed-carry permits, then we could end those Muslims before they walked in,"[11] Jerry Falwell Jr. said in an address to thousands of undergraduates at Liberty University in Lynchburg, Virginia, in December 2015, tapping into a climate of Islamophobia following then presidential candidate Donald Trump's call for a Muslim ban after a deadly mass shooting in San Bernadino.[12] This raw and hateful flex and disgraceful moment came from a leader of an institution of higher education robomarketing itself as Christian. And what are robots usually met with by those of us in the system? Silence. No one within the "Prayer Trade"[13] and Liberty's peer institutions spoke out. Pastors, pundits, and politicians gave Jerry Falwell Jr. a free pass after he intoned this hate speech. They are still at large and in charge.

In another institution and inspired by her undergraduate students, however, Dr. Larycia Hawkins, the first tenured Black woman at Wheaton College and associate professor of political science, spoke up. She also paid a heavy price.

Her subject and theme, then and now, is what she terms, "embodied solidarity." And as a form of Advent devotion, she joined her female students in donning a hijab to counter Falwell's campaign of hate. On December 10, she posted a photo of herself with a head covering on Facebook (a post that has since been taken down) and included a righteously straightforward explanation of her position:

> I stand in human solidarity with my Muslim neighbor because we are formed of the same primordial clay. . . .

> I stand in religious solidarity with Muslims
> because they, like me, a Christian, are people
> of the book. And as Pope Francis stated last
> week, we worship the same God.[14]

A cascade of trolls came for her. Among them Franklin Graham.[15] We all have our robots.

And with the trolls the administration of that self-proclaimed Christian institution, Wheaton College, responded with swiftness. Dr. Hawkins was placed on administrative leave and denied the opportunity to administer final exams.[16]

Despite this blow, Dr. Hawkins made every effort to address her incensed interlocutors within and beyond the peripheries of Wheaton:

> I love you with the power of the love that
> saved me and keeps me and bids me do justice
> to my body.
> . . . As far as it depends on you, will you
> accept my holy handshake?"[17]

As the film covering these events, *Same God*, discloses, this included answering, in writing, a series of questions put to her by Wheaton's administration. When she met with the provost, she was told her responses were, above and beyond, sufficient. But she was also informed that another meeting, on the subject of her faith commitments, was necessary.

Dr. Hawkins did not accept that further, private inquiry concerning her theology was necessary or appropriate. In time, she would be out of a job.[18] When sought by the film's director for an interview, neither the provost nor the president nor the Wheaton College Board of Trustees were willing to be interviewed.[19] It's a tale of prophetic courage, retaliation, and buried conscience hidden in plain sight.

Dr. Hawkins's experience with Wheaton, which commanded headlines for a few months across 2015 and 2016, is a nexus of missed opportunities and warning signs of what was to come. She tapped in when others with less to lose tapped out. In December 2015, she was the most important political science professor in the world. And she invited the world into her classroom.

When the story of her social media post first broke, many held their breath in hopes that Wheaton would stand by her, advancing the evangelical tradition it claimed and eschewing the fear, contempt, and enmity reflected in Jerry Falwell Jr.'s outburst. When Wheaton dismissed her, I remember thinking, *Another robot, another failure of the Bonhoeffer test.* Wheaton, the institution, refused to follow—or even countenance—the moral lead of one of its own.

Theoretical Solidarity Is Not Solidarity

Imagine where we might be now if Dr. Hawkins's institution had had institutional courage to move the needle. If the robots of donors hadn't called the shots. Institutional cowardice, we know all too well, is tyranny's air supply.

"Who are you going to be in the face of injustice?" is Dr. Hawkins's question. It's at the heart of embodied solidarity.

"Theoretical solidarity is not solidarity," she tells us—it's a cruel con: critically detached, a brutal fantasy.[20]

Dr. Hawkins chose the prophetic task of embodied solidarity over silence. When it mattered (it always matters), she bucked the beyondist impulse and overcame deferential fear. Embodied solidarity is the human future that was and is and will be.

Dr. Hawkins and I first met on video in 2017 when my brother-in-law, Jon Foreman of Switchfoot, moved by the martyrdom of Heather Heyer in Charlottesville, felt compelled to facilitate a public conversation online on the subject of white nationalism. I'm ashamed to say that this was the first time it occurred to me to say publicly that white nationalism is antichrist. I have endured nothing comparable to the threats and trauma Dr. Hawkins has experienced since standing up to terror, but appearing in that video and having the conversation marked the beginning, for me, of being the target of people hiding within anonymous social media accounts.

Yet it ennobled and humanized me. Since that time, I've invited Dr. Hawkins to speak at Belmont twice, and she's honored our community profoundly by accepting. In public and casual conversations with our students, she demonstrates a lively intellectual hospitality, an unending wit, and a constant determination to hold the door open for avid inquirers, which I've tried to model ever since. "The function of freedom," Toni Morrison tells us, "is to free somebody else."[21] This is second nature for Dr. Hawkins. She makes it plain. The work of prophetic imagination is an open table to which everyone is invited.

In public settings, I've heard her tell her audience that she wants to encourage them to be prophets, describing what she means and offering the imperatives:

> When I think about the prophetic books of scripture, what's clear is that you can't say you're righteous unless you're also living and embodying justice. . . . Contemporary prophets . . . [didn't just speak] truth to power, they put their bodies in proximity in the places of the greatest injustice in the world. . . .
>
> I think we're called to risk our lives . . . standing up for justice in public ways and private spheres. It can be dangerous. You think about most of our American prophets—many of them lose their lives because their fight for solidarity took a toll on their body, or they're assassinated for the kinds of things

they do . . . the things they say . . . the kinds of responses they arouse. . . . I try to, when I'm in the midst of college students, remind them of their privilege, but also remind them not to be paralyzed by it. Whatever position they find themselves in . . . to use their relative privilege on behalf of the most vulnerable. What I mean by "on behalf of" is amplifying the voices, amplifying the bodies, putting them in a position to speak for themselves.[22]

Despite the price she's paying even now, she has no doubt that she did what was necessary: "I have no regrets," she says. "I would do it again and again and again."[23]

We are always making our witness in one way or another. Dr. Hawkins invites us to weigh out the choices we're making, which make the cultures others will have to live with. She's unwilling to reduce her life to the size of robots primarily designed, in her phrase, to "placate platinum donors." She also notes the distance between authentic faith and advertising ("They didn't give me Jesus and they won't take him away from me.").[24]

There's a serious spiritual resolve here that's essential to discerning that we're normalizing through silence or through remaining in particular spaces. Discerning the spirits and the nature of the robots we're moving in and out of is a deep soul work as well as a creative practice. I think of the "holy handshake" Dr. Hawkins extended online and see how it's still extended even now with good humor coupled with hard-core hospitality. Thanks to her witness, more avenues to authentic humanness are now open.

By her example, we are shown what the prophetic task involves and what it costs. By choosing her own voice, her own prophetic call, again and again at every turn, Dr. Hawkins shows us that we can too. Where robots demand loyalty, flesh and blood invites humanity's voice. Voice is sometimes a heavier but always more liberating task.

Loyalty, after all, is never a virtue in itself. Like faith, it depends on context. It needs a referent. Loyalty to what, exactly? Faith in what, exactly? Fellow human, only you know exactly what it is that you're agreeing to that you don't want to agree to anymore. Is this thing on?

Time and Conscience

"I've come to realize the fear of being cut out from the group of people you respect, and whose respect you want and normally expect, that keeps people participating in anything—no matter how terrible."[25] Do you know the feeling? Can you *feel* the experience of deferential fear in these words uttered by Daniel

Ellsberg, the artisan of moral seriousness who leaked what came to be known as the Pentagon Papers. He is a famous overcomer of what Reality Winner speaks of as the bystander effect. That's when citizens forget that their first job is to govern themselves and to then consider what horrors they're abiding by remaining silent and inactive.

Not everyone is prepared to risk losing the respect they've come to expect in their context.

Not everyone is ready to talk about who they are and where they're at and how remaining a mere bystander does so much harm in our beautiful world.

Reality Winner has appeared in these pages already as a person of deep conscience betrayed by the United States government. Reality houses and invites us to think honestly about our own contradictions. She's like a living, scandalously truthful symbol at the heart of the American fairy tale. I wish the American bandwidth had as much room for her as it does for Donald Trump. Time and conscience are the great revelators.

The fact that this decorated veteran's life appears to be beneath the interest of so many remains a puzzler to me. Her one wild and precious life has been forcibly obscured and overlooked among our robots, missing in the constellation of competing interests, platforms, and brands that control the narratives of the American barnyard. Our risk aversion equals her crushed spirit, as her involvement in our drone pro-gram renders her a human being indefinitely con-signed to dwell outside the sphere of what we're willing to know about ourselves. Not unlike soldier suicides.

Now that she's out (though not allowed to travel past a two hours' drive from her Texas home or break her 10:00 p.m. curfew),[26] she's a unique resource for thinking through our responsibilities to one another within our military-industrial-entertainment-incarceration complex. She has said she looks for-ward to "the day when compassion meets strategy."[27]

Since I saw news of her arrest while I was get-ting my oil changed, she's continually on my mind, more so since she surfaced anew years ago for me, as I was in a different context, visiting Cape Town, South Africa. I took a ferry over to Robben Island where, most famously, Nelson Mandela served most of his twenty-seven-year sentence. There I was shown a small structure where the activist-philosopher Robert Sobukwe was kept in soli-tary confinement for six years. His free speech was deemed so dangerous by white supremacist authorities in South Africa that he wasn't allowed to speak to anyone. This got me thinking about Reality. What is it about her experience and the word of her testimony that's incentivized so many to turn their backs on her?

I recall John Lewis's last testament: "When you see something that is not right, you must say something. You must do something. Democracy is not a state. It is an act."[28]

Plausible Deniability

Reality Winner has been released from prison. Yet it would not be right to say that she's free. By that I mean this: while proponents of the Big Lie can hold press conferences, speak to journalists, film themselves doing and saying whatever they want, and tell their stories freely in any context, Reality Winner, activist philosopher and decorated veteran, cannot. It would be good and proper for Joe Biden to publicly apologize to her and her family on behalf of our government, to pardon her, and to offer her the Congressional Medal of Honor. It would also be appropriate for her to testify before Congress.

Plausible deniability, I've come to sense, is a form of perceived power. From what I can tell, there isn't an elected official (local, state, or federal) in these United States who's felt comfortable publicly acknowledging Winner's existence. With two exceptions. Alexandria Ocasio-Cortez once acknowledged her in an interview, and Justin Amash called on Donald Trump to release her.

Reality's out of prison, but she isn't completely free until she can tell her own story on her own terms.

Having corresponded with her a little and now having conversed with her via Zoom, I've come to find out she's a prison abolitionist whose personal testimony concerning the myth of healing violence is invaluable. Her read on our situation is deeply in sync with that of Anthony Ray Hinton.

Let's recall Claudia Rankine's words: "If you don't name what's happening, everyone can pretend it's not happening."

There's an awful lot happening. If we don't name what's happening, we (everyone) can pretend it's not happening. And what's happening will keep happening until we stop normalizing silence and paying obeisance to our fears and our robots.

What happened to Anthony Ray Hinton?

Someone else's fear happened to Anthony Ray Hinton. The fear and reactivity of others, systematized over centuries, happened to Anthony Ray Hinton. It's still happening. Let's call it the culture we created that happened to him.

But listen: if we don't see and sense the cult in culture, if we don't see all the cults in making a culture and the cultures within cultures, robots within robots, then we can't change. Something has been cultivated in our time together in this book. Something is being cultivated right now. Is this thing on?

We're cultures sitting in and saturated by cultures. There are as many cultures as there are people. I represent more than a few. I contain multitudes, and so do you. As I've said before, ask not if you're in a cult. Ask which ones. Examine and interrogate them. Start with fears and other feelings.

Depending on where we're sitting, standing, and drawing breath, there is a system. Or, if you've been caged in Alabama on death row, you might refer to the system with the kind of authority Anthony Ray Hinton does. Recall what he did and is doing: he's conjuring cultures within and despite the system.

Anthony Ray Hinton once threw me by saying the system is not, in fact, broken. It's doing, he told me, exactly what it was designed to do. It was designed to enslave Black people.

This is Reality Winner's read as well. When pushed on the question of abolition (*All* prisons?), she smiled and had this to say: "Let me put it this way, our prison system is an extension of the transatlantic slave trade. End that, and we can start over with what prisons can and should be."[29]

Anthony Ray Hinton told me the Klan didn't go anywhere. They just changed their white robes for the black ones of the "justice" system.

Fight the system. Love the people. Name what's happening.

8

Spirit Knows No Division

The healing game of infinite play

"Who are you, alone, yourself and nameless?" This is a question I purloined from Stephen Colbert,[1] who borrowed it from J. R. R. Tolkien's Tom Bombadil.[2]

Sit with this lovely, lonely question before reaching for context.

Sit with it alone. Yourself. Unarmed. Robotless. Statusless. No position with which to be identified. No authorization. Nobody telling you what you are.

I was teaching high school English in Nashville when a parent tried to get me fired for declining to say the Pledge of Allegiance. Before it got to that point, the parent and I had a phone conversation that I'd believed settled things. Having aired the concern to an administrator, the parent had been given my phone number. By trying to talk our potential conflict out privately as a first step, we were now in compliance with the school's policy derived from the counsel of Jesus of Nazareth: "If another member of the church sins against you, go and point out the fault when the two of you are alone" (Matt 18:15 NRSVA).

As we concluded, I said I'd love to talk more as time permitted. He said he'd be up for that so long as it was "in the right spirit." I felt a chill and realized then that I had very little control over what spirit (or attitude) he sensed in anything I did or said. He could characterize our exchange to others in any way he wanted to. As it turned out, he was done submitting to conversation as equals. While pursuing his case against me, he would not agree to speak with me about the thing I didn't do that bothered him again. I feared I was now at his mercy. I began to see that meaning can prove fragile. It is, after all, a consensual activity. At that stage in my teaching career, I had more than one superior committed to protecting me and crediting my word as a reliable witness of what I had and hadn't done or said. I kept my job. As I've gotten older, I've tried to remember that millions of people around the world who are targeted by those who are prepared to bring them down do not have that advantage.

I hadn't thought of that conversation in years, but it's come back to me since the domestic terror attack occurred at and within our nation's Capitol on January 6, 2020. A number of people I have known and even loved for much of my life are waking up and wondering if something they've said or played along with can be meaningfully (or legally) tied to a white nationalist terror putsch still, it seems, underway. Declining to platform, support, fund, or partner with citizens and elected officials who have incited or participated in a white supremacist terror putsch isn't divisive, hateful, or an instance of cancel culture. It's what we owe one another. Every fact is a function of relationship. In a nation of equals, assuming responsibility for your own words and actions, especially when they prove to have been demonstrably abusive, is one actionable way of loving your country.

Of course, this love has to begin with particular people, a neighbor, for instance, before it can be said to apply to a city, a state, or a nation. Whether you're a citizen, pundit, or an elected official, you're faced with the question of scope regarding the content you've created or promoted for whatever reason. We become what we promote, mediate, and abide. "I didn't mean that" is of limited usefulness when it comes to assuming responsibility.

Are we responsible for the lies we've allowed other people to voice in our presence unchallenged? We become what we normalize. You bet we are.

Repentance is changing your mind and letting your words and actions follow. It isn't a defeat. It's a moral breakthrough. And it benefits the self and others. It might mean less power to control your fellow creatures, a cut in income, or even a prison sentence, but true repentance is never bad news.

As it happens, "repent" is the first word of Jesus's gospel (Matt 4:17). According to more than one sacred tradition, the wholeness of a genuinely undivided life requires owning your own words and behavior in relationship to others, which will always involve change. To love a person is to love a process and to know oneself *as* a process.

In Tennessee, many a famous person in and out of office claims to be a man or woman *of faith*. "Faith," in this sense, is a best-selling generalization that can win elections, garner followers, and accrue "clicks" in our reaction-driven economy. "Faith," the generalization, can be easily defanged with a simple question: Faith in what, exactly?

When it comes to those who wish to exercise power over others, this question bears repeating. It's imperative to ask it of those who cave and conform to an escalatingly abusive culture that's been slow to recognize the results of our free and fair elections.

Are they interested in the positions of public service they sought and won? If they regard their offices as mere platforms for some other end that doesn't serve the health and thriving of constituents, we need to know. Where, exactly, does this faith reside?

Repentance. It's a necessarily meek practice. But there's no greatness, no human future—no salvation—without it. It's an invitation to be a human being among human beings, an invitation to know the joy of truly human relationship. In this sense, repentance might be said to be the final human seriousness. The move whereby we begin to step out of our robots to save our own lives. Is this thing on?

"Who are you, alone, yourself and nameless?"

Fire, Passion, and Authority

There's a strange story within a strange story. Think *Game of Thrones*.

There was a man who wanted to rule and saw fit to wipe out the kinfolk he viewed as competition. So he secured permission and had it done, but . . . there was one that got away.

The one that got away broadcast a parable, a kind of commentary on what went down, but also a theory (a thinking) of culture, before making his getaway. The parable went like this:

There came a day when the trees decided they needed a ruler to anoint for themselves.

They said to the olive tree, "Rule us."

The olive tree was not at all interested: "Why would I abandon my oil, treasured by gods and humans, to hold sway over the trees?"

Then the trees approached the fig tree: "Come. Rule us."

But the fig tree could not be bothered: "And give up my role in the deliciousness of fig newtons to sway over trees? No thank you."

So the trees beseeched the vine, "Rule us, please."

But the vine shrugged. "I bring good cheer to mortals and immortals alike. It's a lovely gig. Sway over trees? Not a fair trade."

And finally all the trees approached the bramble. "Be our ruler."

The bramble made it plain: "If you're for real, come shelter yourselves beneath me; but if not, then let fire come out of the bramble and devour the cedars of Lebanon!"[3]

This concludes the parable of the bramble.

I won't claim to have gotten to the bottom of it, but I think it offers a helpful way of thinking through fire and passion and authority and . . . deferential fear.

There's also a word about control (pushing, correcting, managing). I read a mocking tone in the "sway over" parts. It's as if aspiring to reign over someone else is a farce, a silly look, an unworthy desire. Especially when it means abandoning gifts that come naturally and bring pleasure. The *swaying over* other beings, even presiding over them, looks to be an exercise in vainglory. What's more, the bramble's primary function is to serve as kindling for fire. And to entrust oneself—to hand over power to someone who's foolish enough to try to take it up—is to be destroyed by them.

Starhawk would perhaps approve. Those who seek or accept "power-over" doom themselves and others. "Power-with" is sustaining, a self-augmenting pattern of mutual aid. True power is anarchic. It doesn't involve force or compulsion. It plays as it lays. Not chaotic, just not controlled or compelled. When I think of the bramble, I think of my own rage and reactivity. It's in there. Always.

"Who are you, alone, yourself and nameless?"

Think again of the bramble and beyondism and love of wisdom and the subtle poetics of robot soft exorcism. The urge to seize and control through the assertion of will and force is ever with us (power-with), but life and liveliness demand a different path to be discerned anew in every situation, every relationship. And this question holds.

Consider the ancient sense that domination (power-over) only enslaves. But, as the bramble within the story seems to understand, there's an energy that can be deployed and exploited even as it consumes. I'm thinking Heraclitus set down a similar insight here:

"War, as father of all things, and king, names few to serve as gods, and the rest makes these men slaves, those free."[4] For "war," think conflict, passion, contention. Think strife. Strife is the father and king of all. It makes some gods and others men; some slaves and others free.

When I think of this insight alongside the pressure points, the robots, and even the forms White Supremacist Antichrist Poltergeist takes among us on our hot blind earth, I'm reminded of a doubling down in disinformation Marshall McLuhan admonishes against: "The more illusion and falsehood needed to maintain any given state of affairs, the more tyranny is needed to maintain the illusion and falsehood."[5]

If we become what we normalize, *playing at* authority is a serious business. There's a passage from Shakespeare's *King Lear* that directs my thinking. It's moving and funny and quite the theory. It's poetry, so I don't want to insist on a gist, but I believe Shakespeare (via Lear) is telling us that authority is playacting. It is absolutely relative to context, and the context is arbitrary. Domineering authority is a barking dog. Check this out:

Thou hast seen a farmer's dog bark at a beggar? . . .

> And the creature run from the cur? There,
> thou mightst behold the great image of
> authority; a dog's obeyed in office.[6]

Who would want to *sway*, we might say, over others? What a farce it is. There's a sneer in that word "great." And consider the word "office." Imagine the human looking down from the robot eye socket. A dog with a momentary advantage over a poor person. That's authority for you. Why play at such a thing? It's disgraceful.

"Who are you, alone, yourself and nameless?"

We become what we normalize. So we must be very careful what we normalize.

The Social Fact of Play

Back in the heady days of bookstores in American shopping malls, that lively era in which a young adult could enter a Waldenbooks or a B. Dalton and behold a volume of Toni Morrison, Piers Anthony, or a *Star Trek* novelization before venturing into Spencer's, there appeared among us, in 1986, a strange, difficult-to-classify, small paperback called *Finite and Infinite Games*. Consisting largely of aphorisms that gradually connect to offer a persuasive account of the whole of human culture, it would prove to be a kind of slow-motion bestseller over time. Robert Pirsig, author of another beloved volume of the time, *Zen and the Art of Motorcycle Maintenance*, claimed that it added a new pattern of knowledge for the right discernment of existing facts. The text would insinuate its way into the thinking of figures like Stewart Brand, founder and editor of the *Whole Earth Catalog*, and virtual reality pioneer Jaron Lanier.

What's it about exactly? It all comes down to the social fact of play. For its author, James Carse, *we are never not playing* in one way or another. How we play—What are we *in* for? What expectations do we bring, and what invitations are we open to discerning from moment to moment?—looks to be the whole deal. It matters.

Does most of life appear before you as a contest, a competition, a scenario in which you're either or a winner or a loser? Are you a finite player in a series of finite games in which you manage to dominate someone else through the assertion of power or get (and feel) dominated? All manner of psychodrama ensues. Perhaps you've witnessed this spirited behavior in yourself and others. Have you, like me, known that, feelingly, at an intersection, realized suddenly that you've been "seen," and sped off in your shame?

Is there an alternative? You bet. Always and in every situation there remains the possibility of *infinite* play (power-*with*, not power-*over*), being present for the moment, the exchange that creates opportunities rather than shutting them down, the conversation that widens the possibility of insight instead of cutting it off. The infinite player *lives* for the moment another person throws the ball *back*. Infinite play escalates the likelihood of people enjoying one another. It signals a space in which individuals can enjoy their own genius by being perpetually open to the genius of others.

For me, robot soft exorcism is a form of seriously infinite play. Yes, I can have a particular finite end in mind when I approach a person in their suit of armor, but if I won't approach them till I know I can be assured of a particular outcome, I'm not quite open, in that moment, to infinite play. I'm probably a little stuck in a spirit of control, of power-over.

Carse employs various terms to identify this righteous human endeavor—infinite play—on which the survival of the species depends, but one that made it well into our own latest century is that of "the creative." Here's Carse: "The creative is found in anyone who is prepared for surprise. Such a person cannot go to school to be an artist, but can only go to school as an artist."[7] This saying privileges the hopeful intuition of the individual against the idea that creativity (or dignity) is something an organization or an alleged educator or a celebrity can give someone else. Our genius and that of others—like divine nature or Buddha nature—is always already there awaiting today's awakening. We have to overcome the ways we've been trained to doubt the possibility of true inspiration: "To be prepared against surprise is to be trained. To be prepared for surprise is to be educated."[8]

For Carse, the preparation for surprise is available and readily discerned in every corner of the human barnyard, regardless of how it is we've been trained to boundary it all up (politics, entertainment, religion, literature). He refers to it as "the mysticism of ordinary experience," which serves as the subtitle of his other most celebrated volume: *Breakfast at the Victory*. The book is a living testimony of how one might somehow study and specialize in researching sacred traditions with a critical eye while persisting in living out the insights handed down to us by poets, philosophers, seers, and other pioneers of infinite play.

He recollects, for instance, a hunting expedition with a friend from seminary following a New Testament class. An avid bird-watching Presbyterian, Carse consented to join an Episcopalian comrade in an effort to assert a degree of manliness. He thusly describes the moral realization that came to him at the sight of a red-breasted merganser he brought down with a rifle: "I overrode a vision of beauty with a need to prove something about my manhood. Instead of quietly beholding what showed itself around me in all the colors of its mysterious otherness, I acted against its natural spontaneity, reducing it to a dull mass. This . . . was an expression of spiritual arrogance."[9]

Can you hear the confession here? The succumbing to the power-over? The bramble?

Embodied Particularity

There is actually an authority at work in infinite play. But it's a poetic authority (prophetic, too, if you like). I believe there are questions that help us do this work. Calling out to the poet within. Questions like these:

- What do I want to see happen?
- What shall I bring—how I shall I mean— today and the next day?
- What shall I do with the fact of the beauty I behold in myself and others?
- How shall we respond to the genius we discern?

In the high anxiety of our everyday new cycles, an ordinary and responsive mysticism that opens up meaning instead of closing it down might be just the thing. I have more impressions than answers to these questions.

In the spirit of that weird parable, I recall a bit of graffiti I once beheld in Cape Town, South Africa: "MAKE A TANGLED BANK."

I like the sound of that. It evokes root systems and tendrils and relation and nuance over robots and divisions and compartmentalizations. It puts me in mind of spirit. And the fact that spirit knows no division. Here's how Darwin writes of the tangled bank:

> It is interesting to contemplate an entangled bank, clothed with many plants of many kinds, with birds singing on the bushes, with various insects flitting about, and with worms crawling through the damp earth, and to reflect that these elaborately constructed forms, so different from each other, and dependent upon each other in so complex a manner, have all been produced by laws acting around us.[10]

Not far from that graffiti is St. George's Cathedral, where Desmond Tutu's ashes are interred and where a jazz club—the Crypt, which also houses the Memory and Witness Centre—is located. St. George's is a holy site to me for a number of reasons, but primary among them is the fact that it's where Tutu—following a discernment process involving ordinary and responsive mysticism alive to the interplay of different but dependent constructed forms—was ordained as the archbishop of Cape Town in 1986. It would be almost eight years before an election open to all races would occur in South Africa. But a beautiful Black man was appointed as leader in the Anglican Communion in the land of his sojourn. Across the street from St. George's ("the People's Cathedral"), there's a piece of the Berlin Wall (a gift presented to Nelson Mandela by a German ambassador in 1996), which invites passersby to imagine these struggles as one unified effort, a tangled bank of love and peace and other higher laws, if you will.

This is also where Larycia Hawkins's vision of embodied solidarity can be spied in Tutu's own public decisions as he sought to honor the trust placed in him, his own sense of self-respect, and the bright but also sometimes brutal fact that association is currency. I have in mind here his friendship with Tony Blair. How does one maintain a morally coherent witness amid the tangle of for-profit disinformation, brinkmanship passing for statecraft, and the managing of egos? How do we keep our relationships in play?

In what looks to me like a commitment to the insight that we become what we sit still for, Tutu publicly refused to share a stage at a "leadership" summit with Tony Blair in view of the fact of his publicly false witness concerning "weapons of mass destruction" in Iraq and the unnatural catastrophes it had engendered. He would not, out of politeness, normalize the behavior of men in ties who treat their fellow human beings as brute-force test subjects. In his commitment, above all, to loving specificity, Tutu knew how to thread a needle: "My appeal to Mr Blair is not to talk about leadership, but to demonstrate it. You are a member of our family, God's family. You are made for goodness, for honesty, for morality, for love; so are our brothers and sisters in Iraq, in the US, in Syria, in Israel and Iran."[11]

Is it possible to respect a person while also lovingly spurning them? Absolutely. We owe it to one another to see past the beyondist armament, the robots in which we're often encased, and look affectionately and sometimes riskily at the human form within. We mustn't speak of or regard one another as abstractions or treat our connections as transactional. Our humanity is a gift. Attending to it, we can be made whole. Tutu goes before us.

I recall, too, William Carlos Williams's adage, "No ideas but in things,"[12] and how Wendell Berry elaborates on this:

> When Williams set down plainly his manifesto, "No ideas but in things," he was not being odd or silly or unintelligent. . . . He was accepting a limit (for himself and his own work, first of all) that would protect things from the limitlessness of abstract ideas, abstract definitions, abstract rules and cases.

Things—or, by implication, persons, places, and things—properly mark the limits of ideas. Things do not merely make manifest the general names and categories by which we describe them; they also impose a discipline upon those generalities, so that the generalities do not become so general as to be unknown and unfelt in embodied particularity—so that they do not, so to speak, escape imagination and form. . . . Concern for ideas in the absence of a concern for things, or at the expense of things, is capricious and dangerous both to things and to ideas.[13]

Tutu, Darwin, and Berry each commend the kind of deep awareness of our own relational situatedness—an embodied particularity—that can overcome reactivity. Both bring to mind the contemplative practices and actions I've heard Larycia Hawkins recommend to her students. Without it, we cave to something less than our most righteous sense of self. Or, as she puts it, "Fear takes over because we haven't done the internal soul work."[14]

The soul work, the meditative task of finding center and bringing to the surface our most playful, poetic, and responsive selves in our world of busy intersections when we feel belittled, shut down, or silenced, is perhaps our most essential task. In taking it up, I'm heartened by a passage from Jane Austen in which Emma Woodhouse is flustered but also on the threshold of a developmental breakthrough:

> How to understand it all! How to understand the deceptions she had been thus practising on herself, and living under!—The blunders, the blindness of her own head and heart!—She sat still, she walked about, she tried her own room, she tried the shrubbery—in every place, every posture, she perceived that she had acted most weakly; that she had been imposed on by others in a most mortifying degree; that she had been imposing on herself in a degree yet more mortifying; that she was wretched, and should probably find this day but the beginning of wretchedness.
>
> To understand, thoroughly understand her own heart, was the first endeavour.[15]

I've tried to set down what I'd like to think of as my developing understanding of the reigning deceptions, within and without, in our heady but sometimes hopeful present. Having been personally talked out of myriad abusive postures and positions, I offer my study (so far) of how this phenomenon occurs in the hope of contributing to the activity of moral integration myself. I don't know my own heart, but I agree with Austen and Emma that trying to understand it is probably the first endeavor—the internal soul work—that can occasionally, like love, overcome fear. This is the healing game of infinite play.

Let's have at it together. May our loves overcome our fears.

Acknowledgments

I've had all kinds of help in this effort. My direct friends and family have watched me try to make the most of my anxieties since the morning of November 9, 2015 (11/9), they have my thanks for their support and they know who they are. There are, however, many writers, editors, and fellow educators who've offered counsel and encouragement when I was feeling awfully alone and somewhat isolated from public discourse. I speak of "writers" broadly because I have in mind many who've published books as well as those who've risked more than a little by letting their names and their faces appear next to the words they've posted on, as the term has it, social media.

W. H. Auden spoke of showing an affirming flame. It seems to me there's more than one way of doing that. I've lost the public approval of more than a few in recent years, but I've gained a number of not-at-at-all-remote friends who've engaged, approved, and amplified my content and helped me find publishers for my work. I think specifically of Heather Havrilesky and Nathan Schneider. I think, too, of editors like Maria Browning of *Chapter 16*, Josh Jackson of *Paste*, and Zac Davis of *America* magazine. Discerning readers of what I set down publicly will note that many of the ideas that show up here appeared in these spaces first. I sometimes think health and wholeness and the overcoming of deferential fear come to us one affirming nod at a time. Whatever coherence comes through in these pages owes much to those who've held me aloft with affirmation and penetrating questions. That goes double for those who appear in my classroom as, at least technically, students. I also want to thank Whitney Bak for sparing me all kinds of embarrassment through her copyediting and, most of all, Lil Copan for bringing this project to fruition with love, care, and insistence. And finally, thank you, Dorothy Day Dark, for all the different expressions that appear on your face and all the healing interruptions you offer as I read my words out loud in your presence. They are a form of sustenance to me.

Notes

Introduction

1 "Patti Smith, 'You Light Up My Life,' on 'Kids Are People Too,'" interview by Michael Young, aired 1979, on ABC, video shared by postingoldtapes, December 9, 2006, on YouTube, https://www.youtube.com/watch?v=Agl4lvNnQPo.

2 Parker J. Palmer, *Healing the Heart of Democracy: The Courage to Create a Politics Worthy of the Human Spirit* (San Francisco: Jossey-Bass, 2011), 76.

3 Fanny Howe, *Night Philosophy* (Brussels: Divided, 2020), 11.

4 Christina Edmondson (@DrCEdmondson), "I ask PWI orgs, 'How do you maintain your whiteness?' so they can acknowledge their decisions," Twitter, August 13, 2022, 6:21 a.m., https://twitter.com/DrCEdmondson/status/1558428 454152019968?s=20.

5 Patti Smith, *A Book of Days* (New York: Random House, 2022), xi.

6 Smith, xi.

Chapter 1

1 Some ideas from this chapter first appeared in David Dark, "Why Are Republicans Sticking with Trump? Peer Pressure—and We're All Susceptible to It," *America*, November 12, 2020, https://www.americamagazine.org/politics-society/2020/11/12/republicans-donald-trump-peer-pressure-election.

2 Daniel Victor, "'Access Hollywood' Reminds Trump: 'The Tape Is Very Real,'" *New York Times*, November 28, 2017, https://www.nytimes.com/2017/11/28/us/politics/donald-trump-tape.html.

3 Jake Sherman, "Ryan 'Sickened' by Trump, Joint Appearance Scrapped," POLITICO, October 7, 2016, https://www.politico.com/story/2016/10/paul-ryan-donald-trump-comments-women-wisconsin-229307.

4 Kenza Moller, "Who Were the Women at Trump's Press Conference About Bill Clinton?," Romper, October 9, 2016, https://www.romper.com/p/who-were-the-women-at-trumps-press-conference-about-bill-clinton-20058.

5 Zeke J. Miller, "Donald Trump Meets with Bill Clinton Accusers Before Debate," *TIME*, October 9, 2016, https://time.com/4524362/donald-trump-bill-clinton-accusers-debate/.

6 Betsy DeVos, "Nomination of Betsy DeVos to Serve as Secretary of Education," full committee hearing (Washington, DC: Dirksen Senate Office Building, January 17, 2017), video shared by the U.S. Senate Committee on Health, Education, Labor and Pensions, 3:56:55, https://www.help.senate.gov/hearings/nomination-of-betsy-devos-to-serve-as-secretary-of-education.

7 Alec Baldwin, "Paul Manafort's House Cold Open—SNL," aired November 4, 2017, on NBC, video shared by *Saturday Night Live*, November 5, 2017, on YouTube, 2:43, https://www.youtube.com/watch?v=spkfIpPmPgs&t=4s&ab_channel=SaturdayNightLive.

8 Toni Cade Bambara, preface to *The Black Woman: An Anthology* (New York: Mentor, 1970), 7.

9 Kurt Vonnegut, introduction to *Mother Night* (New York: Random House, 1966).

10 Donald Trump, "Trump Tapes," interview by Bob Woodward, February 7, 2020 and March 19, 2020, quoted in Quint Forgey and Matthew Choi, "'This Is Deadly Stuff': Tapes Show Trump Acknowledging Virus Threat in February," POLITICO, September 8, 2020, https://www.politico.com/news/2020/09/09/trump-coronavirus-deadly-downplayed-risk-410796.

11 Dina Temple-Raston, "In Touch with Reality Winner," The Record, February 22, 2022, https://therecord.media/in-touch-with-reality-winner/.

12 bell hooks, *Teaching to Transgress: Education as the Practice of Freedom* (London: Routledge, 1994), 12.

13 Ursula K. Le Guin, *The Dispossessed* (New York: Harper & Row, 1974), 149.

14 Merton to James Forest, February 21, 1966, in *The Hidden Ground of Love: The Letters of Thomas Merton on Religious Experience and Social Concerns*, ed. William H. Shannon (New York: Farrar, Straus & Giroux, 1985), 294.

15 Henry David Thoreau, *Walden* (New York: Thomas Y. Crowell, 1910), 11, https://www.google.com/books/edition/Walden/yiQ3AAAAIAAJ?hl=en&gbpv=0.

Chapter 2

1 Some ideas from this chapter first appeared in David Dark, "In the Age of Trump, Can Mr. Rogers Help Us Manage Our Anger?" *America*, April 19, 2017, https://www.americamagazine.org/politics-society/2017/04/19/age-trump-can-mr-rogers-help-us-manage-our-anger.

2 "Harmony Hall," Spotify, track 2 on Vampire Weekend, *Father of the Bride*, Spring Snow, 2019.

3 "The King Philosophy—Nonviolence 365°," The King Center, accessed January 30, 2023, https://thekingcenter.org/about-tkc/the-king-philosophy/.

4 "Box Full of Letters," Spotify, track 3 on Wilco, *A.M.*, Sire, 1995.

5 "A to G," Spotify, track 1 on Blackalicious, *A2G EP*, Quannum Projects, 1999.

6   Lupe Fiasco, interview by Cornel West, at the Festival of Faith and Music (Grand Rapids, MI: Calvin College, April 3, 2009), MP3 audio, 18:15, shared by *Calvin College Student Activities Office* (podcast), April 8, 2009, https://archive.org/details/podcast_ffm-2009_lupe-fiasco-interview-by-corne_53063471.

7   Octavia Butler, *Kindred* (Boston: Beacon Press, 1979), 83.

8   Butler, *Kindred*, 118.

9   William Blake, "London," 1794, Poetry Foundation, https://www.poetryfoundation.org/poems/43673/london-56d222777e969.

10 "Loser," Spotify, track 1 on Beck, *Mellow Gold*, DGC Records, 1994.

11 Butler, *Kindred*, 140.

12 Gilbert K. Chesterton, *Orthodoxy* (New York: John Lane Company, 1908), 85, https://www.google.com/books/edition/Orthodoxy/p7UEAQAAIAAJ?hl=en&gbpv=0.

13 For a film that unpacks the righteous core of this poem beautifully and with direct reference to the text, I recommend *Amsterdam*, directed by David O. Russell (Los Angeles: 20th Century Studios, 2022).

14 Fred Rogers, Senate hearing on PBS funding, May 1, 1969, video clip aired November 22, 2019, on MetroFocus, shared by PBS, https://www.pbs.org/video/mister-rogers-goes-washington-ycjrnx/.

15 Rogers, 2:00.

16 Rogers, 4:11.

17 Rogers, 5:13.

18 Rogers, 5:21.

19 John Lewis, Andrew Aydin, and Nate Powell, *March: Book One* (Marietta: Top Shelf Productions, 2013), 6–7.

20 Mary Oliver, *Winter Hours: Prose, Prose Poems, and Poems* (New York: Ecco, 2000), 37.

Chapter 3

1   William Blake, *Jerusalem*, ed. E. R. D. Maclagan and A. G. B. Russell (London: A. H. Bullen, 1904), 77, https://

www.google.com/books/edition/Jerusalem/h504AQAA
MAAJ?hl=en&gbpv=0.

2 Donovan McAbee (@donovanmcabee), Twitter, September 27, 2022, 7:37 a.m., https://twitter.com/donovanmcabee/status/1574755110512721920.

3 Peter Elkind with Doris Burke, "The Myths of the 'Genius' Behind Trump's Reelection Campaign," ProPublica, September 11, 2019, https://www.propublica.org/article/the-myths-of-the-genius-behind-trumps-reelection-campaign.

4 Jeanette Winterson, *12 Bytes: How We Got Here. Where We Might Go Next* (London: Jonathan Cape, 2021), 73.

5 Socrates, quoted in Plato, *The Apology of Socrates*, trans. D. F. Nevill (London: F. E. Robinson, 1901), 77, https://www.google.com/books/edition/The_Apology_of_Socrates/cJ_nkyjUxNgC?hl=en&gbpv=0.

6 William Blake, *The Marriage of Heaven and Hell* (Boston: John W. Luce, 1906; Project Gutenberg, 2014), 22, https://www.gutenberg.org/files/45315/45315-h/45315-h.htm.

7 LeBron James (@KingJames), Twitter, August 26, 2020, 2:37 p.m., https://twitter.com/KingJames/status/1298721240748711936.

8 Portions of this material appeared previously in Paste Magazine and reappears with its permission.

9 Kenneth Garger, "Jacob Blake Handcuffed to Hospital Bed Despite Paralysis, Father Says," *New York Post*, August 27, 2020, https://nypost.com/2020/08/27/jacob-blake-handcuffed-to-hospital-bed-despite-paralysis-father/.

10 Robert Chiarito, Julie Bosman, and John Eligon, "Jacob Blake Shooting: No Charges Against Officer in Kenosha, Wisconsin," *New York Times*, January 5, 2021, https://www.nytimes.com/2021/01/05/us/jacob-blake-kenosha-rusten-sheskey.html.

11 LeBron James (@KingJames), Twitter, accessed March 6, 2023, https://twitter.com/KingJames.

12 Ashley Boucher, "Pro Athletes Including WNBA, MLB & MLS Players Join Bucks' Boycott Protesting Jacob Blacke's Shooting, *People*, August 26, 2020, https://people.com/sports/milwaukee-bucks-boycott-playoff-jacob-blake-shooting-nba-postpones-games/.

13 Doc Rivers, "Doc Rivers Delivers Emotional Speech on Jacob Blake," video shared by Bleacher Report, August 25, 2020, on YouTube, 0:16, https://www.youtube.com/watch?v=XhqKda79Lys.

14 William C. Rhoden, "Lebron James, Doc Rivers Lead NBA Boycott over Jacob Blake's Shooting," aired August 6, 2020, on MSNBC's *The Beat with Ari Melber*, video shared by MSNBC, August 6, 2020, on YouTube, 5:00, 6:34, https://www.youtube.com/watch?v=BT7vxVh-Oec.

15 *Margaret Attwood: A Word after a Word after a Word Is Power*, directed by Nancy Lang and Peter Raymont, Hulu, 2019.

16 LeBron James, "LeBron James on Jacob Blake Shooting: 'We Are Scared as Black People in America,'" Yahoo! Sports, August 25, 2020, https://sports.yahoo.com/lebron-james-jacob-blake-shooting-164607853.html.

17 Peter Thompson, "LeBron James Hopes Protests during NBA Restart Keep 'Our Foot on the Gas' for Social Change," Sporting News, July 31, 2020, https://www.sportingnews.com/us/nba/news/lebron-james-nba-restart-protests/f782omr1wwq21atp81f17pyw2.

18 Gabriel Fernandez, "Mets, Marlins Observe 42-Second Moment of Silence Before Walking Off Field and Postponing Game," CBS, August 27, 2020, https://www.cbssports.com/mlb/news/mets-marlins-observe-42-second-moment-of-silence-before-walking-off-field-and-postponing-game/.

19 Ariana Freeman, "Ole Miss Football Team Walks Out of Practice to Protest Racial Injustice," CBS News, August 28, 2020, https://www.cbsnews.com/news/ole-miss-football-team-walks-out-of-practice-to-protest-racial-injustice/.

20 Matthew Choi, "NBA, Players Association Agree to Turn Arenas into Polling Places," POLITICO, August 28, 2020, https://www.politico.com/news/2020/08/28/nba-to-turn-arenas-into-polling-places-404457.

21 William Shakespeare, *Troilus and Cressida*, ed. William J. Rolfe (New York: American Book Company, 1905), 3.3.175, https://www.google.com/books/edition/Troilus_and_Cressida

/KYh-Oko3K8QC?hl=en&gbpv=0. References are to act, scene, and line.

22 Claudia Rankine, *Just Us: An American Conversation* (Minneapolis, MN: Graywolf Press, 2020), 169.

23 1 Cor. 12:10.

24 Wendell Berry, *Home Economics* (Albany CA: North Point Press, 1987), 56.

25 "Limelight," Spotify, track 4 on Rush, *Moving Pictures*, Anthem, 1981.

26 Brittany T. Paschall (@btpaschall), "There are holes in this cause empires will empire AND this is important," Twitter, October 6, 2022, 4:07 p.m., https://twitter.com/btpaschall /status/1578144891212734466?s=20&t=s6u51J42e7cE -lUuFOXltw.

Chapter 4

1 W.E.B. Du Bois, *Darkwater: Voices from within the Veil* (New York: Harcourt, Brace & Howe, 1920), 30, https://www .google.com/books/edition/Darkwater/FYpAwPv895kC? hl=en&gbpv=0.

2 Thoreau, *Walden*, 128.

3 Bishop John Franklin White and Bishop McKinley Young, *Episcopal Statement*, Council of Bishops (Chicago: African Methodist Episcopal Church, January 31, 2017), https:// ame-church.com/wp-content/uploads/2017/01/Episcopal -Statement-Council-of-Bishops-re-Trump-Actions.pdf.

4 Anthea Butler, *White Evangelical Racism: The Politics of Morality in America* (Chapel Hill, NC: University of North Carolina Press, 2021), 140.

5 Butler, *White Evangelical Racism*, 144.

6 Billy Graham, quoted in Butler, *White Evangelical Racism*, 34.

7 Butler, *White Evangelical Racism,*106.

8 Jerry Falwell, interview with Pat Robertson, September 13, 2001, in *The 700 Club*, quoted in Butler, *White Evangelical Racism,* 105. See also "Falwell Apologizes for Placing

Blame," ABC News, September 20, 2001, https://abcnews
.go.com/GMA/story?id=126698&page=1.

9 Charles W. Mills, *The Racial Contract* (1997; repr., Ithaca: Cornell University Press, 1999), 18.

10 Mills, 18.

11 Victor LaValle (@victorlavalle), Twitter, June 10, 2020, 6:36 p.m., https://twitter.com/victorlavalle/status/1270877499904479232.

12 Michael Eric Dyson, *Tears We Cannot Stop: A Sermon to White America* (2017; repr., New York: St. Martin's Griffin, 2021), 100.

13 Arthur C. Brooks, "The Culture of Contempt," in *Ways of Knowing*, 7th ed. Daniel Schafer, (Nashville: Belmont University, 2022), 50.

Chapter 5

1 Gene Sharp, *The Politics of Nonviolent Action*, part 3, *The Dynamics of Nonviolent Action* (1973; repr. Manchester, NH: Extending Horizons Books, 2006), 455.

2 Avi Selk and Sarah Murray, "The Owner of the Red Hen Explains Why She Asked Sarah Huckabee Sanders to Leave," *Washington Post*, June 25, 2018, https://www.washingtonpost.com/news/local/wp/2018/06/23/why-a-small-town-restaurant-owner-asked-sarah-huckabee-sanders-to-leave-and-would-do-it-again/.

3 Kathryn Watson, "Sarah Sanders Says She Was Asked to Leave Restaurant Because She Works for Trump," CBS News, June 23, 2018, https://www.cbsnews.com/news/sarah-sanders-says-red-hen-virginia-restaurant-owner-told-her-to-leave-2018-06-23/.

4 Ramsey Touchberry, "Sarah Huckabee Sanders Service Refusal Compared to Racial Segregation as Protests Greet Red Hen Reopening," Newsweek, July 6, 2018, https://www.newsweek.com/protests-red-hen-opens-denying-sarah-sanders-1012653.

5 Wendell Berry, *The Need to Be Whole: Patriotism and the History of Prejudice* (Berkeley: Shoemaker, 2022), 30.

6 Eph 6:12 KJV.

7 CPD Action (@CPDAction), "WATCH: '@senatemajldr why do women have to bare their whole soul to you and share their stories & you won't listen?' @traceycorder caught Majority Leader McConnell," Twitter video, October 1, 2018, 12:30 p.m., https://twitter.com/CPDAction/status/1046829 665736957952?s=20&t=ZwHd62rFeZdwaNl8oclWAA.

8 Maria Gallagher, "I Was in the Elevator with Jeff Flake. Senators, Don't Look Away from Me," *New York Times*, October 4, 2018, https://www.nytimes.com/2018/10/04/opinion/brett -kavanaugh-confirmation-vote.html.

9 Greta Thunberg, "School Strike for Climate: Meet 15-Year-Old Activist Greta Thunberg, Who Inspired a Global Movement," interview with Amy Goodman, *Democracy Now!*, December 11, 2018, https://www.democracynow.org/2018/12/11 /meet_the_15_year_old_swedish.

10 Sarah Freeman-Woolpert, "Meet the Activist Who Brought the Monopoly Man Meme to Life," Waging Nonviolence, December 12, 2018, https://wagingnonviolence.org/2018/12 /meet-the-activist-who-brought-the-monopoly-man-meme -to-life/.

11 Starhawk, *Truth or Dare: Encounters with Power, Authority, and Mystery* (1987; repr., New York: HarperCollins, 1990), 84.

12 Marc Halpin (@marc_halpin), "I am learning from and valuing David's use of specificity in his writing. I think specificity causes people to pause," Twitter, July 9, 2020, 10:19 a.m., https://twitter.com/marc_halpin/status/12812616419513180 18?s=20&t=ZwHd62rFeZdwaNl8oclWAA.

13 David L. Ulin, "Claudia Rankine, The Art of Poetry No. 102," *The Paris Review* (Winter 2016): https://www.theparisreview .org/interviews/6905/the-art-of-poetry-no-102-claudia -rankine.

14 Paraphrase of Matt 25:42–43, quoted in Spencer Buell, "Religious Leaders Confront Jeff Sessions in Boston: 'I Call on You to Repent,'" *Boston*, October 29, 2018, https://

www.bostonmagazine.com/news/2018/10/29/jeff-sessions
-boston-bible-verse/.

15 Buell.

16 Buell.

17 Buell.

18 Howe, *Night Philosophy*, 101.

19 George Stephanopoulos, *Good Morning America*, interview
with Sarah Huckabee Sanders, aired April 19, 2019, on ABC,
video shared May 1, 2019, in Cheyenne Haslett and Lucien
Bruggeman, "5 Key Takeaways from Special Counsel Robert
Mueller's Report," ABC News, https://abcnews.go.com
/Politics/key-takeaways-special-counsel-robert-muellers
-report/story?id=62493619.

20 James Blish, *A Case of Conscience* (New York: Ballantine,
1958), 14.

21 Martin Luther King Jr., "Love, Law, and Civil Disobedience"
(address to the Fellowship of the Concerned, 1961), quoted in
Richard Wayne Wills Sr., *Martin Luther King Jr. and the Image
of God* (New York: Oxford University Press, 2009), 146.

22 Daniel Berrigan, *Lamentations: From New York to Kabul and
Beyond* (Chicago: Sheed & Ward, 2002), 77.

Chapter 6

1 Claudia Rankine (commencement address, Wesleyan University, Middletown, Connecticut, May 28, 2017), transcript
accessed in Lauren Rubenstein, "Rankine Delivers 2017
Commencement Address," *Wesleyan Connection*, May 28,
2017, https://newsletter.blogs.wesleyan.edu/2017/05/28
/rankine-delivers-2017-commencement-address/.

2 Jessica Hopper is a friend with whom I've discussed these
matters. When I put the question to myself, I hear it in her
voice because she posed a related question ("Who do you
excuse and why?") in her essay "Where the Girls Aren't,"
Rookie, July 13, 2015, https://www.rookiemag.com/2015/07
/where-the-girls-aren't/2/.

3 Grace Paley, *Just as I Thought* (1998; repr., New York: Farrar, Strauss & Giroux, 2014) 191–92.

4 Kimberlé Williams Crenshaw, "The First Decade: Critical Reflections, or 'A Foot in the Closing Door,'" in *Crossroads, Directions, and a New Critical Race Theory*, ed. Francisco Valdes, Jerome McCristal Culp, and Angela P. Harris (Philadelphia, PA: Temple University Press, 2011), 20.

5 Ibram X. Kendi, *Stamped from the Beginning: The Definitive History of Racist Ideas in America* (New York: Nation Books, 2016; repr. New York: Bold Type Books, 2017), 10–11.

6 "Marian Anderson Sings on the Steps of the Lincoln Memorial," History, last updated April 6, 2022, https://www.history.com/this-day-in-history/marian-anderson-sings-on-the-steps-of-the-lincoln-memorial.

7 Christopher Mele and Patrick Healy, "'Hamilton' Had Some Unscripted Lines for Pence. Trump Wasn't Happy," *New York Times*, November 19, 2016, https://www.nytimes.com/2016/11/19/us/mike-pence-hamilton.html.

8 Ric Hudgens, "Possibly Even Magic," Radical Discipleship, October 9, 2020, https://radicaldiscipleship.net/2020/10/09/possibly-even-magic/.

9 My sources here include my notes from Bree Newsome's "Tearing Hatred from the Sky" (public lecture, Vanderbilt University, Nashville, TN, March 22, 2016), which was recorded and can be viewed on YouTube, https://www.youtube.com/watch?v=gVQekde_res), and Rebecca Butts, "Daughter of Freedom Center's Leader Removed Flag in S.C.," *USA Today*, June 29, 2015, https://www.usatoday.com/story/news/nation/2015/06/29/south-carolina-confederate-flag-removed-activist/29454101/.

10 White and Young, *Episcopal Statement*. They quote Eph 6:12 KJV.

11 Roland S. Martin, "Crazy A$$ Man Sings 'Dixie,' Harasses & Threatens Black Tenn. Commissioner During Press Conference," June 6, 2021, in *#RolandMartinUnfiltered Daily Digital Show*, produced by Black Star Network, YouTube video, 1:40, https://www.youtube.com/watch?v=_JvEnd_pkzA.

12 Tami Sawyer (@tamisawyer), Twitter, June 7, 2021, 9:34 a.m., https://twitter.com/tamisawyer/status/140192558182714 9829.

13 Christina Edmondson (@DrCEdmondson), Twitter, August 19, 2021, 9:02 a.m., https://twitter.com/DrCEdmondson /status/1428371925202579456?s=20&t=B7rOo_KBrpv -_bgpievgUQ.

14 Svetlana Boym, *The Future of Nostalgia* (New York: Basic Books, 2001), xiii, xvi.

15 Sanders, *Fug You*, 88.

16 James Baldwin, *I Am Not Your Negro: A Major Motion Picture Directed by Raoul Peck* (New York: Vintage Books, 2017), 107.

17 James Baldwin, "Many Thousands Gone," in *Notes of a Native Son* (1955; repr., Boston: Beacon Press, 2012), 25.

Chapter 7

1 "United States Supreme Court Grants Relief to EJI Client Anthony Hinton," Equal Justice Initiative, February 24, 2014, https://eji.org/news/us-supreme-court-grants-relief -anthony-ray-hinton/.

2 Anthony Ray Hinton, *The Sun Does Shine: How I Found Life and Freedom on Death Row* (New York: St. Martin's Press, 2018), 10.

3 Hinton, 11.

4 Hinton, chap. 14–15.

5 James Baldwin, *Go Tell It on the Mountain* (New York: Alfred A. Knopf, 1953; repr., New York: Vintage International, 2013), 110, quoted in Hinton, 150.

6 Hinton, 156.

7 Hinton, 155.

8 Hinton, 164.

9 J. C. spoke these words to me when he was in eighth grade and I was conducting a philosophy club in a classroom at J. T. Moore Middle School, circa 2019.

10 Václav Havel, "The Power of Powerlessness," 1978, on the Hannah Arendt Center for Politics and Humanities (website), Bard College, December 23, 2011, https://hac.bard.edu/amor-mundi/the-power-of-the-powerless-vaclav-havel-2011-12-23.

11 Sarah Pulliam Bailey, "Jerry Falwell Jr.: 'If More Good People Had Concealed-Carry Permits, Then We Could End Those' Islamist Terrorists," *Washington Post*, December 5, 2015, https://www.washingtonpost.com/news/acts-of-faith/wp/2015/12/05/liberty-university-president-if-more-good-people-had-concealed-guns-we-could-end-those-muslims/.

12 Jessica Taylor, "Trump Calls for 'Total and Complete Shutdown of Muslims Entering' U.S.," NPR, December 7, 2015, https://www.npr.org/2015/12/07/458836388/trump-calls-for-total-and-complete-shutdown-of-muslims-entering-u-s.

13 David Dark, "Nashville's Entangled 'Prayer Trade' Is a Warning to the Rest of the Country," Religion News Service, October 20, 2022, https://religionnews.com/2022/10/20/nashvilles-entangled-prayer-trade-is-a-warning-to-the-rest-of-the-country/.

14 Ruth Graham, "The Professor Suspended for Saying Muslims and Christians Worship One God," *Atlantic*, December 17, 2015, https://www.theatlantic.com/politics/archive/2015/12/christian-college-suspend-professor/421029/.

15 Franklin Graham, "Both my father Billy Graham and my mother attended Wheaton College in Illinois—in fact that's where they met," Facebook, January 23, 2016, https://www.facebook.com/FranklinGraham/posts/1082008785188635/?paipv=0&eav=AfYLP_hL6OtYiDQ_P_E0wV2kPssDlS-UwZRqqf_xQzsgd3Dhmc4vr1FYSkjE44Tkoil&_rdr.

16 Chris Pleasance, "Evangelical Christian College Professor Who Vowed to Wear a Hijab for the Holidays and Declared 'Muslims and Christians Worship the Same God' Is Suspended, *Daily Mail*, December 16, 2015, https://www.dailymail.co.uk/news/article-3363090/Evangelical-Christian-college-professor-vowed-wear-hijab-holidays-declared-Muslims-Christians-worship-God-suspended.html.

17 Larycia Alaine Hawkins (@larycia), Facebook, "This morning, I partook of the Eucharist, the culmination of the Christian liturgy where Christians through the centuries have united around a common table," December 13, 2015, https://www.facebook.com/larycia/posts/10153331120918481.

18 *Same God*, directed by Linda Midgett, staring Larycia Hawkins (2018), DVD.

19 Emily McFarlan Miller, "Controversy over Wheaton Professor's Hijab Captures Evangelical Rift in New Film," Religion News Service, October 4, 2018, https://religionnews.com/2018/10/04/controversy-over-wheaton-professors-hijab-captures-evangelical-rift-in-new-film/.

20 Larycia Hawkins (speaker, First Year Seminar Ambassador Speaker Series: Transformative Justice, Massey Performing Arts Center, Belmont University, Nashville, TN, October 28, 2022), hosted by David Dark.

21 Toni Morrison, "Cinderella's Stepsisters" (commencement address, Barnard college, New York, 1979), transcript accessed in ZORA Editors, "Toni Morrison: 'I Am Alarmed By the Willingness of Women to Enslave Other Women,'" Medium, August 7, 2019, https://zora.medium.com/toni-morrison-in-her-own-words-562b14e0effa.

22 Amanda Haggard, "Professor Who Was Forced Out of Wheaton College Talks Trump, Evangelism," *Nashville Scene*, February 1, 2018, https://www.nashvillescene.com/arts_culture/features/professor-who-was-forced-out-of-wheaton-college-talks-trump-evangelism/article_3f94a55d-f63c-5e59-9522-cd8a2cc2f185.html. Reprinted with permission.

23 Haggard.

24 *Same God*, 41:32.

25 Daniel Ellsberg, *The Most Dangerous Man in America: Daniel Ellsberg and the Pentagon Papers*, directed by Judith Ehrlich and Rick Goldsmith, first aired October 5, 2010, on PBS, re-aired January 7, 2018, on MSNBC, 1:37:00.

26 Reality Winner, Zoom call with author, October 21, 2022.

27 Douglas Lucas, "Reality Winner Sentenced to 63 Months," *The Public*, August 24, 2018, http://www.dailypublic.com/articles/08242018/reality-winner-sentenced-63-months.

28 John Lewis, "Together, You Can Redeem the Soul of Our Nation," *New York Times*, July 30, 2020, https://www.nytimes.com/2020/07/30/opinion/john-lewis-civil-rights-america.html.

29 Winner, Zoom.

Chapter 8

1 Joe Hagan, "'Look at What We Love. It's on Fire': Stephen Colbert on Trump Trauma, Leadership, and Loss," *Vanity Fair*, December 1, 2020, https://www.vanityfair.com/hollywood/2020/11/stephen-colbert-on-trump-trauma-leadership-and-loss?utm_brand=vf&utm_social-type=owned&mbid=social_twitter&utm_source=twitter&utm_medium=social.

2 J. R. R. Tolkien, *The Fellowship of the Ring* (1954; repr., William Morrow: 2022), 131.

3 Judg 9:1–15, author's paraphrase.

4 Heraclitus, *Fragments*, trans. Brooks Haxton (New York: Penguin Books, 2003), 29.

5 Marshall McLuhan, preface to *The Mechanical Bride* (New York: Vanguard, 1951), vi.

6 William Shakespeare, *King Lear*, ed. Horace Howard Furness, vol. 5 (Philadelphia: J. B. Lippincott, 1880), 4.6.152–56, https://www.google.com/books/edition/King_Lear/xVwJAAAAQAAJ?hl=en&gbpv=0.

7 James P. Carse, *Finite and Infinite Games: A Vision of Life as Play and Possibility* (1986; repr., New York: Free Press, 2012), 56.

8 Carse, 19.

9 James P. Carse, *Breakfast at the Victory: The Mysticism of Ordinary Experience* (1994; repr., New York: HarperCollins, 1995), 137.

10 Charles Darwin, *On the Origin of Species* (London: Cassel, 1909), 413, https://www.google.com/books/edition/On_the_Origin_of_Species/d9biAAAAMAAJ?hl=en&gbpv=0.

11 Desmond Tutu, "Why I Had No Choice but to Spurn Tony Blair," *Guardian* (US edition), September 1, 2012, https://

www.theguardian.com/commentisfree/2012/sep/02/desmond-tutu-tony-blair-iraq.

12 William Carlos Williams, "Book 1" in *Paterson*, rev. ed. (1992; repr., New York: New Directions Books, 1995), 6.

13 Wendell Berry, *The Poetry of William Carlos Williams of Rutherford* (Berkeley, CA: Counterpoint, 2011), 95.

14 Hawkins (speaker, First Year Seminar Ambassador Speaker Series: Transformative Justice), hosted by Dark.

15 Jane Austen, *Emma*, vol. 2 (London: Ward, Lock, 1881), 369.